I0389516

Calling Humanity

Third Edition

Copyright© 2002, 2004, 2021 Jose Trigueirinho Netto

The profits generated from sales of books by Trigueirinho and his associates will be used to support the non-profit activities of the Shasti Association to disseminate their work.

Original Title in Portuguese:
UM CHAMADO ESPECIAL

Cover photo and artwork:
Clovis Loureiro and Columba (Cláudia B. Miranda)

Translation and revision:
John David Cutrell and Yatri (Frances O'Gorman, Ph. D.)

Cataloging-in-Publication data

Trigueririnho Netto, Jose
Calling Humanity
168 p.
Trigueirinho. - Mount Shasta, CA, Shasti Association 3rd edition
ISBN:978-1-948430-02-9
Library of Congress Control Number: 2021930539
1. Spirituality
2. New Age
3. Occult Science
I. Title.

English language rights reserved

Shasti Association
P.O. Box 318
Mt. Shasta, CA 96067-0318
editorial@shasti.org
www.shasti.org

A Cosmic Event Is Taking Place

INFORMATION FOR THE NEW TIMES
BY
TRIGUEIRINHO

Calling Humanity

Third Edition
Revised by the author

Introduction by
Carol E. Parrish-Harra, Ph. D.

Organized and edited by
Artur de Paula Carvalho

Contents

Introduction — The Future Stands Revealed,
by Carol E. Parrish-Harra, Ph. D. vii

To the Reader xvii

PART ONE

The Meeting 3

In the Valley of Erks 7

A Message from an Earlier Civilization 15

The Greatest of the Mirrors of Light 25

Presences That Make Themselves Known 37

The Transfer of Planetary Energies 43

The Current Role of Lis-Fatima 47

Incubation or Sleep in the Temple 53

Radiation and Healing 59

The Great Magnetic Network 65

The New Genetic Code 75

Awakening of the Right Side Consciousness 81

PART TWO

Planetary Centers 89

Spiritual Hierarchy 93

Cosmic, Intraterrestrial and Surface Races 95

Space Vessels 99

Our Role Today 103

Choices for Evolution 105

PART THREE

An Exercise to Develop Right Side Consciousness 109

Tasks for the New Human 117

A New Dawn 121

The Future Stands Revealed

An Introduction by Carol E. Parrish-Harra, Ph. D.

José Trigueirinho Netto of Brazil is a remarkable teacher. His personal integrity has earned the respect of the Brazilian public, both secular and those on a spiritual quest. The concepts contained in his seventy books and in the more than six hundred audiotapes recorded live during his talks have inspired the open-minded for years. Stretching the imagination and confounding the intellect, Trigueirinho provides details that expand known horizons to a new spatial depth, inviting us to ponder while piecing together the puzzle of multi-dimensional life. Just as once upon a time Buck Rogers and space travel gripped our attention, although they were cloaked in fantasy, they prepared us for the space age.

To present José Trigueirinho Netto and his futuristic information to the English-reading public, even while controversial, is a challenge I relish. Anyone daring to introduce such a hard-to-believe, far-fetched, easy-to-reject story is at risk. We must also be quite confident of the integrity of the one conveying such revelatory ideas. Thus, the demonstration of dedication, honesty and character of Trigueirinho is brought to our attention. His incredible story can assist us in understanding the subtle world and how to dissolve the blinders that hold us captive to the past. Dare we proceed to be the ones to build the new civilization?

Trigueirinho's broad spectrum of writings in an undisguised language has inspired his audience to expand their thinking. His excited readers anticipate each edition for a greater picture of life, providing an extraordinary collection of futuristic concepts about the formless beings that fill the world around us and interact with some for evolutionary purposes. All of his books have been translated from his native Portuguese into Spanish, and an even greater audience has been thrilled. Until now, however, only a few pieces have made their way into English. Occasionally a special friend or inspired individual would share a favorite selection or memorable paragraph with another, informally translating as they were so moved.

Some twenty years ago José and I began an acquaintance that has touched the lives of world servers worldwide, a few at a time. After inner plane contact, we came to know and respect each other, gathering details and weaving them into our efforts to facilitate the Great Work of this exciting era, as well as advancing the lives of those who are ready to explore the topography of universal life. While some seemingly remain bound to the material, others discover that new frequencies bear a reassuring familiarity. Overcoming limitations and barriers that restrict is the evolutionary effort required to gain vistas beyond the common.

Past wisdom teachers have implied there is an expanded reality, which we are rapidly approaching. Certainly the New Testament speaks of a new heaven and a new Earth, but few take time to ponder what this may mean. We begin again each time we see or perceive in a very different way.

When certain limitations fall away, humanity will begin again, and in this less limited state will remodel personal and collective life accordingly. A degree of lost paradise will be rediscovered, and human consciousness will reestablish a relationship to what are currently considered angelic and spatial beings. More encompassing ideas about Creator, Creation, and our purpose will be natural to that state of mind.

Philosopher Paul Brunton expressed this by saying, "New forms will be needed to satisfy the new knowledge, the new outlook, the new feelings. The classical may be respected, even admired; but the creative will be followed."[1] He also recognized the awareness we are struggling

---

[1] Paul Brunton, The Notebooks of Paul Brunton, Relativity, Philosophy, and Mind, vol. 13, para. 66 [Burdett, NY: Larson Publications, 1987], page 92.

to birth in our era: "Today's need is not merely a synthesis of modern scientific ideas with ancient mystical ones, not merely a dovetailing of Oriental and Occidental teachings, but virtually a new creation to fit the new age now about to dawn."[2]

Heavenly signs and uncertain proof point to the evolving relationship between subjective and objective reality. In like manner it is so for surface Earth beings, inner Earthlings, and the above-Earth existence. Those who know this have had to await a signal to speak out. The time is now.

Trigueirinho is one of a few who has this knowledge and serves by placing these realities within reach of many. Knowing each of us will be empowered as we shift our awareness toward activating our potential and embarking on our path of ascent, he shares generously even that which may be seen as improbable or unprovable.

This incredible work, which began with a little-understood touch of spirit, hidden from most, has filled the life of Trigueirinho with powerful revelations. He has been given many previously unrevealed insights into the workings of the cosmos and humanity's part in it. While we have claimed to be the centerpiece of God's creative handiwork, now we must face the reality that we are but one of a multitude of beings and kingdoms, as we discover that every dimension teems with life forms.

Herein you are invited to experience the richness of a stream of consciousness that traces new, unprecedented conceptions about the cutting edge of impressions of other realities. As one who was introduced to the public by Ruth Montgomery after having experienced a soul exchange, or walk-in transformation, and bearing the endorsement of her guides, I am privileged to further address this behind-the-scenes change Trigueirinho calls "monadic transmutation." He is a messenger of this dynamic shift as well, with full memory of the event and a dedication unmatched for serving at this crucial moment in the collective life.

---

[2] Paul Brunton, The Notebooks of Paul Brunton, Reflections on My Life and Writings, vol. 8, para. 208 [Burdett, NY: Larson Publications, 1987], page 54.

This hard-to-explain event (I call it "soul exchange") is noted in The Masters and the Path [3] wherein he shares H. P. Blavatsky's discussion of another body being prepared for her even as she exhausted the one she was using at the time. Rudolf Steiner spoke of the exchange in The Gospel of St. Luke, stating that one could fall into a dead faint, the Inner Self leave the body, and a new Inner Self take over.

Master Djwhal Khul, the Tibetan, through his amanuensis Alice A. Bailey, used the term "divine obsession" for such an experience. Each of these was guided to share with others a radical method of admittance into physical form to acquaint those who were ready with an unorthodox or an uncommon means of service. This particular event and additional revelations enrich our body of knowledge as we fearlessly penetrate the invisible realms and discover shining eyes watching over us. Barriers to intra-dimensional life are dissolving. These contacts we are having will once again change our picture of the world as we move from a three-dimensional reality to an expanded field of perception.

The exchanges of which I speak are facilitated by the inner world as a way the body, the emotional nature, and mental mechanism can be salvaged from a disappointing life or destructive personality by bringing a wiser being from the subtle plane (some might say "the other side") to replace the original builder of the body. For the karmic lords to approve the exchange, this incoming soul must have a worthy service to perform. Wise ones behind the scene facilitate consciousness and adjust life threads for the benefit of all: the departing one, the messenger coming in, and the well-being of the collective to be served.

Trigueirinho's story is excitingly different from most soul exchanges in that he made contact with an incarnated member of the Hierarchy after he was already a spiritual teacher. The hierarchical contact, Sarumah, came to him, they met, and Trigueirinho was invited to serve as he now does.

---

[3] C. W. Leadbeater, The Masters and the Path [Adyar, Madras, India: The Theosophical Publishing House, 1925].

Sarumah then accompanied him to the Valley of Erks and stayed with him several days and nights as he underwent the necessary changes. Level by level his nature was purified and energetically realigned for the new incoming consciousness that could receive the transmissions now being shared with those who sense something big is happening. The cosmos calls.

Through learning of such events, we acquire a fresh perception of Creation, its work, and its purpose, as well as the phenomena of other planes. Secret observations are materializing from behind the veil of sleep into awareness that rings with recognition. We begin to comprehend deeper meanings preserved in myths and legends that come to us through fairy tales and ancestral storytelling, plus the great truths of ageless wisdom. Now we can assert more strongly there is more to life than we can explore with our physical senses.

While individual work still has to be done, human behavior is being affected by higher impulses seeking to bring us into relationship with the hierarchies of wiser ones. Humanity is predestined to express its "made in the image and likeness" of the divine, nurtured by the feminine influences of Sophia, Maria, Kuan Yin—names we know.

When one has been prompted by the unseen world for decades, one finds daily reality more fascinating than fiction. At the same time, greater numbers are in the process of exploring the world within. Some find themselves encouraged to guide the way to dissolving limitations for the whole and to share their discoveries so we all can ponder divine possibilities.

Trigueirinho has been experiencing the panorama of unseen life since his exchange in 1988. He has walked the tightrope between inner and outer realities, noting event after event of higher contact. His fine mind for detail has recorded his interactions with the unseen. Trigueirinho experiences an enriched reality as he is tutored by contacts from other levels who define the inner workings of heavenly space. Here he views a life filled with beings who find it natural to live in a state of harmony, while we mortals find this hard to comprehend when compared to our Earth's conditions.

It is exciting to realize that contact with other beings and other realms is happening right now. This may be as simple as accepting that angels are indeed watching over us or that the foundations of stories of space beings, inner realities, and inner plane schools are all true—in symbology if not in specifics. These concepts have been whispered for ages, yet here again we find a reputable leader testifying to incredible events. Periodically, such individuals, strong in character and true to their word, are willing to risk reputation and ridicule to open human minds to challenging adventures.

Couched in gentle, clear terms, this story is being disclosed to reassure those who seek to know life is magnificent in its unlimited dimensions. Within its concentric planes we can imagine Jacob's vision of angels descending and ascending the ladder. (Gen. 28:12) Today we have a number of records of contacts with beings—sometimes visible, sometimes not. As we experience the power of new vibrations in so many ways, we begin to realize it may have to do with us whether or not they are perceived, not whether or not they are there.

For over a century, word has emerged that the powerful masculine energy of Shamballa, the center where the will of God is known, is diminishing. Prophecies—by The Tibetan, Brother Philip, and, it is said, even the previous Dalai Lama—revealed energy changes would bring a revitalizing flow to the Andes of South America. Other sources also affirm the withdrawal of the divine masculine and the strengthening of the divine feminine, as well as the center for anchoring the highest incoming energies from the Himalayas to the Andes. Three sets of teachings were promised by the Tibetan. The statement I consider most significant reads:

> I would have you remember that the teaching which I have given out has been intermediate in nature, just as that given by H.P.B. [Helena P. Blavatsky], under my instruction, was preparatory. The teaching planned by the Hierarchy to precede and condition the New Age, the Aquarian Age, falls into three categories:
>
> 1. Preparatory, given 1875—1890 ... written down by H.P.B.
>
> 2. Intermediate, given 1919—1949 ... written down by A.A.B. [Alice A. Bailey]
>
> 3. Revelatory, emerging after 1975 ... to be given on a worldwide scale via the radio.

In the next century and early in the century an initiate will appear and will carry on this teaching. It will be under the same "impression," for my task is not yet completed and this series of bridging treatises between the material knowledge of man and the science of the initiates has still another phase to run.[4] [This I believe to be the work Trigueirinho is delivering today.]

Many acknowledge our world has shifted from a healthy masculine force to an abusive over-reaction. Having reaped the rewards of what the powerful impulse achieved, we now witness as the expression falls into misguided impulses.

At the same time, an ever increasing feminine nurturing stimulus is making itself felt through healing, sensitivity, and a changing society. From the re-emergence of natural healing to leadership in university halls worldwide, the click of a feminine heel is replacing the wing-tipped, heavier step of the more competitive male world. With this incoming wave of energy come concerns and a cry for another way— one more inclusive, more caring, and with more hope. The strong emotionalism of the past is to fade, to be replaced by a more inclusive, unconditional love-wisdom.

Wisdom teachings prompt us to observe rhythms and cycles so that we can integrate the momentous changes that occur with the cosmic movement from one age to another. Progress is made even when little is grasped intellectually, for we learn through emerging experiences. Though we stand knee-deep in chaos at this point, we are scanning the horizon for answers. Trigueirinho's contacts explain humanity's past struggles. Tragically, lack of love and respect for greater life concentrated our efforts on false values and self-importance. This unprecedented information provides avenues of hope for today and for the future.

To grasp an invisible reality that we are being nurtured is not easy; so finding one who will testify to subtle contacts amid the daily confusion brings confidence. This introduction heralds our assistance

---

[4] Alice A. Bailey, A Treatise on the Seven Rays, The Rays and the Initiations, vol.V [New York: Lucis Publishing Company, 1960], page 255.

from a higher plane; it is not to sensationalize but to reassure. In order to reject mounting fears of a changing age and to rejuvenate hearts grown weary, we welcome this guidance. Here the deeper meaning of texts found around the world—originally given to encourage—is revealed.

When I introduce subjects or points of view that surprise or challenge audiences, I suggest they build an imaginary bookcase in which to place uncomfortable concepts. In that way they can choose to look at seemingly questionable perspectives in their own good time. As Victor Hugo said, "There is nothing so powerful, not all the armies in the world, as an idea whose time has come."

As you pursue this material, concepts may come together to provide meaningful ideas or reinforcement for your own experiences. In fact, the inner knower may bring forth a resounding "Yes!" I expect many to experience excited recognition. In fact, inner knowing and faith in the unknown and the unprovable provide a remedy for the toxicity of manipulation, suspicion, and self-doubt of our modern materialistic civilization. The falseness of those who would claim only that which can be explored with our five physical senses is ignorance in itself. Knowing we are so much more, we are now refusing to be limited as we transcend known boundaries and venture into the passion of the cosmos. It is not enough to nurture our grief and sadness with restricted life, but we must support a cause or a belief that addresses it. Beauty and high vision feed the soul; then healing can happen.

Always, stories of unending life have provided whispers of encouragement. Likewise, flashes of light, momentary contacts with invisible realities, and perceptive insights into the nature of life have served as guideposts for those willing to depart the wide smooth road of social structure to adventure upon the path of mystics and the emerging next stage.

People ahead of their times open us to exciting possibilities. Visionaries who catch a glimpse of greater life attempt to share with others what the future holds. Currently, the efforts of both inner workers and outer are focused on preparation for the next evolutionary step. These become the subject of reverence at times, distrust at others. Such people as Trigueirinho continue to provide the markings of the narrow way for those who are advancing both their chakra system and their DNA. They open doors, just as powerful modern shifts promise.

This material, without a particular religious or denominational approach, is radically respectful of the innate quest to be carried to fruition. High consciousness now beckons a change of attitude or destruction. Some doubt there is an answer except to obliterate this civilization and create anew. Others respond with renewed vigor formed by anticipation of fresh revelations. Certainly destruction could prove to be so if we cannot listen to those who are now contacting wiser ones, warning of the dangers we create. Life evolves in the care of those who can see the greater and more refined way toward harmony and cooperation.

Innately, many long for senses that will vibrate to higher influences, or we would not hear of concepts such as ascension, light body, or Christed. Herein is the story of one man's monadic transmutation, the wisdom to which he adheres, the lifestyle suggested by the contacts from spirit/space, leading him and others to build bridges within their bodies to enable them to live divinely. Compare how life changes when one goes from sightless to capable of seeing. So it will be when we of this society release the current consciousness and perceive additional life in other forms already functioning in our space. In this world we are entering we transcend the limitations of this one. Already individuals hesitantly share their angel stories while others stand ready to provide a level of additional insight I find exciting.

The style of this book is unique, as is its purpose. Herein, chapters have been selected to serve as pearls of wisdom strung together, whispering to you across bountiful amounts of information. The greater library of Trigueirinho's seventy volumes awaits translation. Five to ten books are currently being prepared for English readers, but the planetary urgency is great. Every ray of light that can touch a precious mind is now an important one. Trigueirinho's work bears the stamp of true revelation and it echoes in hearts inwardly awakened.

Dare to explore this material, knowing only certain parts have been selected to share. An introduction cannot tell everything. It is designed to entice you to want more. This volume is to inform English readers that even as our challenges are great, there are those who stand with planet Earth, providing hope and offering help from the Earth's surface, from within the Earth, and from more subtle planes. Coworkers from subtler planes as well as embodied workers, reveal themselves with willingness to those who embrace radical change.

Stop for a moment. Listen. Can you detect a sacred sound reverberating through the cosmos? It is so. From Neil Armstrong's first step on the moon for humanity, we have become increasingly ready for this information. With high regard and deep respect, I introduce the works of José Trigueirinho Netto to you, readers in English. Unprecedented horizons beckon.

To the Reader

By Artur de Paula Carvalho

This book has been especially organized for this time of planetary emergency. The chapters have been taken from different volumes of the vast works by Trigueirinho. This cohesive selection of writings offers an introduction to the profound teachings given to us through Trigueirinho.

The information presented here can serve as a doorway through which we may enter as we receive the new evolutionary impulses that are being poured down on humanity in a unique way in these times. The previously unrevealed teachings can only be confirmed in the silence of one's heart, bringing great joy to one's Being as these new seeds are sown.

In the opening pages of one of his books, Trigueirinho offers some insights into how his writings came to be:

> This work is the fruit of the efforts of a group which, on the inner levels of life, acts under the aegis of Hierarchies. It is an answer sent by the Inner World in response to the appeal for teachings. In an ever-fresh manner, these Teachings can point out the path to the Light. They bring seeds of coming times and make them available to those beings whose consciousness is to become fertile ground for the transformations that announce the new Earth.
>
> Those who work as channels that attune to and materialize these texts know they are but intermediaries, and silently express gratitude for the opportunity to serve altruistically.

May the reader who is devoted to the Truth, divested of concepts and expectations, seek the ways of inner revelation. Here he or she will find keys to the portals along this Path.

This is also our wish.

Love and Light to all beings,

Artur and the group of volunteers who
cooperated in this publication
August 2002

Part One

"Certain forces and powers, exterior to the government of the solar system, have been called into play, owing to the planetary emergency. This emergency is of such importance (from the angle of the consciousness) that the Solar Logos has seen fit to invoke external agencies to aid. And, They are aiding."

(Alice A. Bailey, A Treatise on the Seven Rays, vol. II,
Esoteric Psychology [New York: Lucis Trust, 1970], page 450.)

"The truth is that the present crisis has no parallel in history except that which preceded the destruction of Atlantis."

(Paul Brunton, The Notebooks of Paul Brunton, vol. 5,
Emotions and Ethics [Burdett, NY: Larson Publications, 1987], page 227.)

"The Great Brotherhood, these rulers of our planet, were High Spirits on other planets and Men-Gods on our Earth. Belonging to the higher evolution, They came to our Earth in order to accelerate the evolution of its humanity. Indeed, They are, in the full sense of the word, the Protectors, the Guardians, and the Saviours of our planet."

(Helena Roerich, Letters of Helena Roerich,
vol. II [New York: Agni Yoga Society, 1967], page 198.)

The Meeting

Excerpted from: Erks —The Inner World,
by Trigueirinho

A participant of the group approached me after the meditation gathering and said in a low halting voice: "A gentleman wants to speak to you. When can we schedule a meeting?" I answered that I would look over my appointments, but I did not do so right away. The following day the person told me again in the same tone of voice: "He really wants to come. Did you check your calendar for a time to meet?" I went to look at my schedule. Since all the times were reserved for other work, the only available time was at 1:00 p.m. on the coming Wednesday.

Later on I found out that Wednesday at 1:00 p.m. was the ideal time to meet this gentleman, perhaps one of the few times possible. He arrived moments before the meeting. As soon as we entered the room we looked at each other in the eyes. I perceived that we had known each other forever; neither of us even asked anything about the other. Sarumah[1] was simply there, beside the desk, and totally at ease. He had brought some papers and a large envelope that he placed before me. It was as if that meeting had been prepared thousands of years ago. Impressions like this are possible, and because of an intuitive certainty they become reliable, safe and so clear that they leave no room for doubt. When we find ourselves face to face with a being whom

---

[1] Sarumah. A member of the Hierarchy of the planetary center of Erks was incarnate for a number of years to prepare some specific steps in the current planetary transition. Sarumah is also a member of the Alpha and Omega Council, which intermediates the consciousness of the planet with the cosmos.

we have always known, we can identify him without any need for phenomena to ratify it.

The conversation went straight to the essential point of the work that was going to begin. We knew that things have neither a beginning nor an end, as was expressed at a certain moment of our conversation; they have always existed, they do not start nor do they finish, they simply are. Although aware of this state of consciousness outside of the normal human time frame, in that meeting room we experienced the interesting impression that a new cycle seemed to be unfolding. We were happy to take part in this play of time and form. A wave of the energy of Love immediately came over us and we talked about everything that we considered necessary.

I knew of the existence of people like the one standing before me, but up until that time I had not been aware of having been physically in touch with one. Sarumah gave me the impression of having a perceptible inner assurance about everything. I listened to him with my whole being, present and participating there, in both inner and outer dimensions.

That same month we met twice again. We scheduled our next contact for six months later. Then I returned to Brazil where other aspects of the work awaited me. This book[2] began to be written two months after those initial contacts and it was finished in 48 days because of the need to disseminate its content.

Sarumah brought me photographs, written material and a small, illustrated manual containing basic exercises. As this was being placed before me there was not the slightest surprise, because inwardly I had known of it for a long time. However, it was clear that it was the first time in this incarnation that the area of the evolutionary work represented by Sarumah was being brought into my consciousness in this way. It also seemed to be necessary to feel and to live this experience on the physical, emotional and mental levels.

ଓଃଡ

---

[2] This refers to Erks—The Inner World, 1989, turning point for a new phase in Trigueirinho's work.

In the quiet of the dawn my mind would become immersed in a deep receptive state. I could concentrate unreservedly on the subject, and so I dedicated myself intensely to this inner search.

Nowadays changes are rapid, drastic and continuous. Therefore, sometimes an instruction can quickly become outdated. In the esoteric and scientific field, a discovery can soon become obsolete. Thus the teachings offered in this book will most probably be complemented and updated in the future. Bearing this in mind and surrendering to the eternal now, let us go on with our reflections.

In the Valley of Erks

Excerpted from: Signs of Contact, by Trigueirinho

One could say that consciousness, when polarized on the three-dimensional world, is characterized by curiosity. On the other hand, the search for knowledge is a characteristic of the fulfillment of the Plan of Evolution and of each being's task within this plan. Therefore, when we consciously decide to cooperate with the process of purification, as proposed here, and when we open ourselves up to new knowledge, we should let go of our human emotional impulses. We should let ourselves be guided only by the aspiration to become part of the new laws that will begin to govern terrestrial humanity. Up until now humanity has limited itself to the planetary laws that apply to material spheres, such as the Law of Birth and Death.

In the following pages we will be looking at information that is practically unknown on Earth. Therefore, we will be facing unusual experiences. None of this, however, should take us away from an impartial and neutral attitude, an attitude that allows the light from a higher level to bring forth a better understanding in us.

ೞಐ

When I accepted the invitation to go to the Valley of Erks,[1] I knew I would be living through important phases of a purification pro-

---

[1] Valley of Erks. A region in the province of Cordoba, Argentina, where the supraphysical center of Erks projects its energy in a special way.

cess that had already begun in me and I tried to be unconditionally open to it. Beings with experience and wisdom cooperated with this process. Thus, without any conflict or doubt, I prepared myself for whatever might come, no matter how unusual, without the slightest expectation. In a way, I felt like those who in the past had consciously followed the supraphysical path to evolution and were ready to enter the pyramids to receive messages or inner stimulation through higher consciousnesses that worked there to serve the Earth. As we know, at certain cyclical moments of our development we need intermediaries between the higher energies and ourselves.

An ancient Chinese saying came to my mind: "The spirit from the depths of the valley is imperishable."

In a way, the energy that in the past had manifested that message was also present in the valley where I was heading, a valley that to me would be like a pyramid of modern times. To experience this reality was sublime because, according to the above Chinese source of wisdom, "The Perfect Path is ever more precious."

Although it had never crossed my mind, to withdraw from an experience like this would be inconceivable. I clearly saw while awaiting it that "the web of the Heavens is infinite, its nets are wide and no one can escape them." When we reached the place where the valley opened up, we stopped the car and got out. I walked a little and found myself at the edge of a canyon. I did not look down for I was observing the far end where a large light, the coordinating space vessel,[2] was supposed to appear to give us a signal. And it did appear and shone brightly on the horizon, greeting us. Commanded by a great Being, it seemed to be transmitting to me the Tao Te Ching saying handed down from olden times:

---

[2] Space Vessel. A field of cosmic energy in the planet's magnetic field. It brings to Earth higher laws and energies only available in distant regions of the cosmos. As of 8/8/88 (August 8, 1988) more primitive extraterrestrial consciousnesses, such as those that used to visit the planet with the intent of carrying out experiments, have been denied entry to the environs of the Earth.

What is incomplete will be completed,
What is curved will be made straight,
What is empty will be filled,
What is worn out will be renewed,
What is lacking will be increased,
What is excessive will be scattered.

Rituals such as the one that was beginning for us in the Valley of Erks also used to occur in the past. However, today, at the end of a cycle and of a civilization, they have taken on another form, adapted to the present times. The place where we were standing contained no pyramids or dark chambers. Rather, the "ceremony" was taking place in the open air, assisted by the wind, the air and the energy that was everywhere, including in the undulating and radiating mountain skyline. All was peace and harmony even when a strong wind blew across the area. Whenever the wind died down, the sky would become completely clear. "How pure and tranquil is the Path! I know not from whom it comes, for it seems to have existed before the Sovereign of the Heavens," says the eternal wisdom.

The Pleiad[3] who accompanied me throughout this phase of the process said we could go on down by car to get a little closer to the area of contact. It was located on the level of the lower mountains facing the valley. We drove for a stretch, then stopped and waited for another signal. We knew that when the vessels become materialized or arrive from their missions, the magnetic field of a large area is modified by the dynamic energy they emanate. This is why physical approach to these areas must be gradual and under the command of the vessels. The commanders of the vessels control the pulse of the local magnetic field and know well those who are called to undergo certain experiences. If people follow the transmitted signals rigorously, nothing disharmonious will befall them. Deep inside they will feel a serene joy,

---

[3] Pleiad. A general term to designate highly evolved extraterrestrial beings who come from incorporeal regions of the cosmos to help humankind. The term Pleiad should not be confused with Pleiadean, which has a different meaning. In this narrative the Pleiad is Sarumah.

that will expand the receptivity of the conscious self and predispose it to the purification that is so essential today.

We stood there for a few moments before the second phase of physical approach began. Looking around, we could see dozens of vessels that had made themselves visible to assure us of their cooperation on all levels. "Everything is under control," said the Pleiad. I had not doubted it. But it was reassuring to hear it said aloud.

On the horizon ahead, the lighting network of the intraterrestrial city of Erks was beginning to appear before our eyes. So we went on a little farther until we were about a thousand feet from the scene of what was happening. There, we stopped. We knew we could go no farther without permission. The lights of the car were turned off and we were enveloped in total darkness. The intraterrestrial city lay before our eyes so that later I could testify to its existence through the books I was to write, as well as the contacts I would have with others who were interested.

૦૩૮૦

I spent ten nights in the Valley of Erks: two consecutive nights at the beginning of the month, three others at the end of the same month and another five nights some twenty-five days later. On only two of these nights the Pleiad was not physically there with me, apparently because he had other matters to attend to. However, I learned afterwards that his absence was really to prepare me to remain there in the future without his presence, whether for a few hours or for an entire night.

When I returned to the capital city where a busy time of public meetings awaited me, my friends remarked that I had changed very much. I explained that I had gone through a kind of healing and that my emotional body, above all, had been worked on inwardly by positive energies that were aware of my evolution.

I felt a new vibration circulating through me. Even if I tried, I could no longer feel emotions as before. The deep sense of inner union, of receptiveness, of gratitude and peace never left me. In this way I spent three weeks as if time and space had become rarified. They were without weight, without gravity, without any form of attachment. Each of my public lectures brought the confirmation of the great inner unity that existed with everything and everyone. The wave of energy that flowed through me and through what I said, was different now. People noticed it and referred openly to it as transformation. Even so, none of this was emphasized or dramatized. Life went on normally, though many knew that I had been in contact with the Valley of Erks.

The events that took place in the Valley of Erks prepared my higher self to set up an effective link between physical and astral-emotional consciousness. From then on, all emotional activity could be intelligently controlled. My mind, in turn, was able to expand its capacity, establishing a link between its thinking area and its abstract area. This latter is what some classical books of spiritual philosophy refer to as the over-mind. Expansions of light from supra-mental levels were already shining through the soul, the higher self. In outer life, service was to be expanded, and this is what affected my temperament most of all.

For those around me then, being with me was a training. They observed subjective events becoming manifested on the physical plane. Meanwhile, I was going through some tests in order to adapt to a new awareness and viewpoint. New energies became more intense within my consciousness and the synthesis of my Lemurian past was being brought back into my awareness. In it I found many liberating keys for the present time. During those studies I realized how useless all previous psychological analyses had been.

What happened on the following nights, back in the Valley of Erks, cannot be narrated in chronological order. The description of time, of the rhythm of the days, of states of consciousness, follows an inner movement and not a mental sequence.

Having the Law of Purification in mind, during one of our car trips to the valley, I said to the Pleiad, "I don't know how to explain this, but I know I will be going through a great transformation." "Yes," he answered promptly, "it won't be long now."

While we were driving along an unpaved road, a space vessel accompanied us in the sky to my right. I looked at it and greeted it, saying to the Pleiad, "If it is to happen, I am ready." "Yes, it will happen," he repeated, and began chanting mantras as he drove.

We reached the top of the mountain and got out of the car. I put on a robe the Pleiad had given me to wear that night or on any other night of vigil. On the physical plane, everything was set. On the inner planes, I felt a detachment such as I had never experienced before. Usually one thinks that when the time comes for transmutation, one has difficulty in letting go of earthly things. This did not happen to me. Even as it became absolutely clear that my inner being would be living the experience of transmigration to other planes and to other worlds beyond this solar system, no part of me offered resistance. I was serene and at ease with no sign whatsoever of discomfort.

And thus it happened: the inner being departed, without the human consciousness being at all aware of it. I stood there, sometimes talking to the Pleiad, other times listening to what he said or chanted. I watched the vessels that were helping this process but never thought about myself, about what might happen, or what might already be happening to me. Total security and peace encircled me.

I suddenly realized that a great distance separated my human consciousness from the one who had always inhabited my body, or the bodies known to my ego. Yes, there was a physical distance of light-years between the individual observing and the one who, unnoticed, had departed on a long journey. For a moment, I kept very still inwardly; nevertheless, I never felt alone or left on my own.

The Pleiad then told me that the inner being who had just transmigrated had fulfilled his tasks here on Earth and was therefore liberated. As he said the word "liberated," I felt great joy. I was participating in the joyful incorporeal state where he who had inhabited these bodies now was. Thus I realized that physical distances do not mean much.

I did not know where the inner being that I had known as the main part of myself during my whole life, had gone, yet I felt no separation. "The one in you now has a more expanded consciousness. This helps your conscious human part to be able to see more broadly," said the Pleiad. Yes, it was quite clear to me that this was not due to any merit of my physical aspect or of my personality. Everything was due to supraphysical levels, mine and those of cosmic beings who were giving us signs of their presence all around.

"Everything is under control," said the Pleiad. "Do you feel any discomfort?" "None," I replied, "there is only a small spot on the right side of my neck which seems a little sensitive, that's all." The Pleiad kept repeating, "Everything is under control." And we looked up at the vessels.

Thus occurred the transmigration of the inner being who had inhabited my physical-emotional-mental sheath for a certain period, and the transmutation of the inner being who will inhabit this sheath until a certain task is completed. During transmutation, the physical body and the conscious self felt nothing at all, remaining lucid at all times. After that, when I concentrated my human mind more intensely on the center of my being, I noticed there was another energy there. "You are going to notice it more clearly as days go by," said the Pleiad, smiling. "Little by little you will get to know it better." However, it seemed as if I knew it very well, as though I had known it before. Then I saw that mystery is always present. Our union was so deep that I almost forgot my inner self had left and had gone on its way to another experience. Aware of this, I could feel nothing but gratitude growing within. Yet this gratitude not only arose from within, it also came from "afar," across many light-years.

I watched the vessels around us and deeply sensed the help I had received. My physical eyes saw the night sky covered with stars and vessels many light-years away. What are distances? What do they mean? All was well and peace reigned within and outside my being.

A Message from an Earlier Civilization[1]

*Excerpted from: Miz Tli Tlan —An Awakening World,
by Trigueirinho*

"To your world:

"It would be good to underscore the fact that there are three types of worlds and even though integration of their civilizations has always been desired, their inhabitants have never truly related to one another. These worlds are: the extraterrestrial world of the cosmos, the intraterrestrial world of the hollow Earth and the world of its surface. The world where you are on the surface of the Earth[2] is moving rapidly toward the destruction that our ancestors also could not avoid, and that once turned planet Earth into a hideous gigantic tomb full of corpses, ruin and desolation.

"All this happened at a very remote time, way beyond your conjecture. At that time humans witnessed the events that were taking place but could do nothing. Each civilization reaches a maximum point of development and then immediately or gradually disappears. It is

---

[1] Sarumah obtained this information from hermetic societies in North America and Argentina.

[2] World of the surface of the Earth. From here on the term "of the surface" will always mean the surface of the Earth.

consumed like the stars. Universal life is an eternal mathematical game, composed of cycles that contain certain annihilating aspects.

"Our technological development had reached impressive levels of perfection. Even at astonishing distances we were able to break down matter into units of energy and also reconstruct it. The effects of the radioactive residue were kept under control.

"This practice brought about the use of disintegrator plants (or stations), where machinery could transform a physical form into energy and project that energy to any city on the Earth, where another machine would transform that energy back into the same form. It later became commonplace for individuals to have their own machines.

"There were practically no secrets for us.

"Thanks to our scientific knowledge we could do almost anything we wanted to, including to extend life indefinitely. This was made possible by using the process of hibernation, which our social system allowed. Hibernation consisted of having our vital functions suspended for years and later simply taking a pill to return to active life.

"The governing class had managed to correct the problem of the agglomeration of living creatures. It was able to control the excessive growth that had occurred in the population and its resulting contamination. Evidently, lengthy periods of time were needed for everything to be adjusted because our peaceful nature did not allow us to adopt any aggressive measures against those who transgressed the norm.

"In the assistance centers the newly born received programming pills that produced the effect of curbing any violent action against a fellow being.

"Nevertheless, serious problems began to arise due to the lack of growth in consciousness regarding continual technological progress. On a memorable date the governing council finally thought up a solution for these problems. In order to avoid death, from then on we had to have governors with total decision-making power. They then programmed a new race that cooperated with the plan of evolution. Prepared to look beyond both the bad and the good, they legislated with extraordinary wisdom. The population growth was limited and under this regime, conception was controlled and prevented.

Furthermore, the decrepit, the senile and those considered to be socially unrecoverable were eliminated.

"But we had been making a mistake. An aberration in the structure upon which we had consolidated the society of the surface went by unnoticed: the motors of our powerful technology were being fueled exclusively by atomic energy. We knew about other forms to produce clean energy but we were satisfied with the degree of security obtained from controlling the splitting of the atom. Evidently, in the beginning we had to deal with the radioactive residue, which we placed in special capsules and then buried. Later we were able to transform that residue and finally we reached what we called the point of a no-loss consumer chain. It could be compared to an engine of today, powered by gasoline, that could continually collect and reutilize all of the gases generated by its combustion. We had reached the point where we thought we had achieved everything when one of our mathematicians warned us that after a certain time (which you would measure in terms of hundreds of years) the spectro-magnetic lines of the recycled energy were unexpectedly no longer responding to the rigid laws they had followed up until then.

"In other words, they rebelled. For, what else could this anarchy of the spectro-magnetic lines of atomic recycling mean? When we found this out, it was too late. Our science had completed its cycle and all of us remembered the wise words of the last philosopher: 'However, death still exists.'

"The radioactive content of the atmosphere began to increase tremendously, producing black holes in the ozone layers that surrounded the Earth. The super-complex machinery that supported the structure of our civilizations rapidly became useless. You must realize that we had constructed real cybernetic monsters, capable of restoring, on their own, the parts of the machinery that had become damaged for whatever reason. Some, therefore, lasted for a longer time and we managed to obtain a regulator for the rate of increase of radioactivity. But this was of little help. We had not bothered to obtain immunity to the radioactivity, which we depended upon totally, just as today you would not go in search of immunity to the water of your rivers, thinking that tomorrow they could be converted into a factor of death.

"We suddenly knew that we were alone and defenseless.

"We had not progressed as a race; on the contrary, we remained at an elementary stage. Without being aware of it, we had simply contributed to the emergence, the splendor and the twilight of super-technology. Technotronics had controlled us.

"We had to flee from the cities. Fortunately, we knew which direction to take and we attempted to carry out the exodus strictly within the directives set by the governors. These same governors had once been obliged to adopt extreme measures to avoid a demographic explosion and had ordered the new cities to be built in four perfect rings around the surface of the planet, going through the area that today is called the equator. One of the things that I must warn you about is that the topography of the planet was different then. At that time the continental platform was a wide strip that covered the space between the tropics, to the south and to the north. In the area where today the poles are located there were upwelling marine currents, which is to say, natural lines of communication placed in the form of a geometric network under the seas. Through them waters came up from the interior of the planet to the surface and then returned.

"Nowadays that network is completely fragmented. The waters come out of the intraterrestrial world and return to it through only four openings. These, according to your cartography, are located in the triangles of Tokyo-Shanghai-Vladivostok, in the sea of Japan; of Sydney-Melbourne-New Zealand, in the Tasmanian Sea; of Malvinas-Río Gallegos-Viedma, in the Argentine Sea; and of Bermuda-San Juan, Puerto Rico-Bahamas, in the North Atlantic Ocean.

"The evacuation of our population was carried out in stages. First those who lived in the inner rings were transferred to the outer ones so as not to wait until the last minute and then be obliged to cross a deadly belt composed of the areas where the laws had been most changed. Meanwhile, desperate efforts were still being made to find a solution. Yet, we did not know what to do, as we had to base ourselves exclusively on our own knowledge, without the support of the artificial brains. The technological brains had even gone so far as to console us when our psychic system suffered from the impact of the upheaval of the situation.

"We had become accustomed to using recyclable matter as a source of energy and we finally came face to face with a reality we had not expected. We did not have the means to use the more primitive forms of energy controlled by the natural laws of matter. We had inadvertently held back the development of consciousness to a technological level of progress and had allowed matter to overrule it.

"What would be the use of trying to return to those sources if we no longer had the devices that could run on those types of fuel? You would understand us if you could imagine yourself being told today to go back to using steam ships. You could produce steam—but where are the ships?

"This is when the crisis broke out. That perfect, super-developed society was nothing more than a parasite on a gigantic technological animal. The only parasite on the only animal. If it died, what would be left?

"Decadence set in rapidly. The capacity to give orders had long depended on complete records of information that foresaw the need and the consequences of the order being given. It had become very difficult for us to think for ourselves!

"Many chose to remain in the cities, defying the rising level of radiation. They soon became distortions of what they had been. They suffered bone deformations, went blind because of eye cataracts, and finally died through lack of motor coordination.

"Those who fled wandered through the jungles which we had never bothered about. They faced unfamiliar animals that were unknown to us because the populated belts were protected by strips of total barrenness. They drank water from the streams and many died because they had lost the genetic coding that allowed them to assimilate water in its pure state.

"Others collapsed while they were eating. They had lost almost all their capacity to adapt to the terrestrial environment. Some gathered together in coordinated cells, attempting to survive what awaited them.

"Special pills gave many the balance that the body needed and only by taking these pills could they be assured that food and water would not turn into their enemies.

"The journey was very strenuous. Super-specialization had caused us to become invalids. However, we continued to stay alive, in spite of the warning of the last philosopher: 'Death still exists.'

"One of our alternatives for survival was to reach the marine sources moved by ono-zone[3] and get to the inner part of the hollow Earth, where we hoped we would not be ravaged by radioactive contamination. Yet, how could we get there?

"How will somebody who lives in Philadelphia and always uses the telephone to communicate with somebody in New York feel when, one day, he or she discovers that no telephones work?

"We wandered through the jungles... Old age caught up with us. We discovered that our existence as senile parasites was miserable. Meanwhile, radiation had reached intolerable levels and the survivors hurried toward the seaboard, searching for the coastlines of the ocean. Enormous cataclysms fragmented the external layer of the Earth into millions of pieces, as if a massive explosion had overtaken our devastated world. Nevertheless, in the midst of this conflagration, our race continued to retain its archetypes.

"By not permitting debilitated couples to procreate, we managed to select four who could serve as reproducers in laboratories, and even in the most inhospitable conditions we managed to have three perfect children generated from them. Raised in the jungles, not knowing the benefits that their ancestors had enjoyed, the little ones began a new society.

"Like us, they spoke very little. We had long given up the spoken language and had chosen brain-to-brain transmission, thanks to the good performance of extra-cerebral receivers provided by the great technological monster that supported us. After that, it was very difficult to start speaking again and some never managed to do so.

---

[3] Ono-zone. The One Cosmic Energy of life, all pervading and omniscient. Ono-zone is absolute harmony and is expressed according to the laws of the universes in which it is being manifested. Prana is a material aspect of ono-zone energy.

"One of the coordinator groups took on the task of telling the story of what had happened to the terrestrials in symbols that were used for communication at that time. This was done in order to pass history down to the new humans who were already starting to have children. A new biological chain began with a shift in the genetic code.

"This is the story of the race of those who live in the depths of the Earth, the race of those who, in order to rise out of the ashes of a civilization, had to bear much more than you have had to undergo. It is told here and could serve as a basis for today's humans, if they wish to take advantage of these experiences.

"While the world on the surface was falling apart through innumerable cataclysms, our civilization began to regenerate, gradually yet surely. The new Earth, inside the planet, bestowed its resources on us in the same way that the previous one had done. However, there was a fundamental difference: it allowed us to start again from a point of no contamination. It was our 'second chance' of which philosophers spoke in the past. It was only then that we realized how important these philosophers were. They knew more than any supermachine and yet we had actually mocked them!

"About four hundred centuries had to go by before we felt we were strong again. We knew that once again we had reached the exact point where the road forked, where those who molded the race had once erred and had begun to proclaim the death of the race. We made good use of this second chance, faithfully following the principles contained in the decalogue that we had inherited from the 'first ones' and which tradition had kept alive. These mandates included things that addressed the experience of past times lived on the surface of the Earth which, for millennia, we had been unable to understand. Gradually, with the advance of a new science, precepts such as, 'Atomic energy is the cause of death and must not be employed' began to make sense to us. The rediscovery we made of the atom unveiled the meaning of this first article, which warned us not to go on with that study.

"This time we chose to look into magnetic force, but we discovered that magnetic fields of a certain intensity cause physical changes in objects and in beings. So we abandoned that system as well and tried others, until we selected the energy obtained from picking up ono-zone photons coming from the stars. These photons reached us from the outside through inter-magnetic channels or holes. Thanks to the knowledge and control of this energy, we were able to penetrate even deeper areas of the planet that we had always considered to be dark. We were thus able to build new cities and finally to suspend the restrictions set on birth control. Our race continued to grow.

"There were always those among us who, stimulated by the philosophers, set out to find the original land, that is to say, the birthplace of our species. They headed for the marine currents, passing through the frozen lands unknown to our ancestors. These lands were the outcome of the ecological disaster caused by our predecessors. They reached the continental soil after having crossed extensive marine areas. According to your cartography, they went through the land of Victoria, going on by sea to New Zealand, and from there to Australia, across Melanesia, after which they arrived in Japan and the coasts of China between Canton and Tientsin.

"Of those who left, few returned. They were mesmerized by the luminosity of the days, by the blue sky, by the sea breezes, by the abundance of the vegetation that offered them fruits without needing to plant, and by the quantity of wild animals available for hunting, a sport that was discovered accidentally and which fascinated them.

"Our governors decided to study the geophysical year of the outside surface with the intention of verifying the conditions there for life to progress. The results were wonderful. It was observed that, for thousands of years there had been no signs of the radioactive eruption that had scathed our ancestors. Nature had slowly but relentlessly eliminated all vestiges of contamination.

"Thousands then decided to leave the inner part of the Earth. As had happened previously in our history, the governors once again had to make an important decision. They forbade us to leave the world inside the Earth. This was done in order to stop us from going back to that point of degeneration that we had reached at the time when we had been humans of the surface. The governors set a time limit for the return of those who had already left. After that they would no longer be re-admitted because they would have even acquired a different physical structure. The unity of the intraterrestrial race was preserved. Those who did not return formed the foundations of the yellow race based in China, Japan, the east coast of Mexico and the southernmost part of Argentina. Prior to that, the population in China was either white or black. The yellow race that we know today has intraterrestrial origins.

"Escape from the intraterrestrial world occurred through the natural conduits under the seas that interconnect the world of the surface with that of the interior of the Earth. But this was being kept under control.

"The geophysical year on the outside had revealed some interesting facts, besides that of the lack of radiation in the environment. We learned that the human race had not disappeared completely from the surface of the Earth but, because of the extensive mutations it had undergone over time, its humans had a slightly different form than ours, as well as radical changes in their physical appearance. We did not find any representatives of the original race there, but we did come across black and white people in a near-animal state, with a very low level of intelligence.

"We were also able to verify that our permanent source of water for the inner rings had remained intact. We are referring to what you call Lake Baikal, in Siberia. Around it we found some colonies of animals bearing almost the same characteristics that tradition assigns to the animals that lived together with our ancestors on the surface.

"Now that a gradual evolution has granted human beings from the surface of the Earth moderate intelligence, they rush headlong into the same trap that caused the destruction of the primordial race. The first step in that direction was the building of the atomic bomb, an artifact with unlimited potential for harm that will serve to create governments of terror, throwing the world into total disaster. This disaster may reach us also, because it is impossible to know how far a confrontation using nuclear weapons can reach.

"We are not about to let this happen. This is why we are warning the world of the surface, through its most significant countries, of this danger. We want them to form an international committee against the use of nuclear energy. In exchange, we are willing to reveal the secret for the utilization of magnetic energy."

The Greatest of the Mirrors of Light

Excerpted from: Miz Tli Tlan —An Awakening World,
by Trigueirinho

Highly evolved beings have been able to enter the realm of energies and are working toward the progress of the worlds. This is the case of those who inhabit Aurora, Erks and Miz Tli Tlan[1] and who cooperate with the evolution of humanity of the surface. Their work is carried out on the subjective levels of life as well as directly on the material planes. However, most human beings know very little about these activities.

In this context, "energy" refers to that which comes from the mother-source, while "force" is the name given to the action that occurs within the material body, the body formed of circuits. The one energy subdivides as it externalizes. All of its parts emanate from the same source, reflect on each plane or dimension and permeate those planes from the highest to the lowest. Thus the one energy is manifested in descending gradations.

The "mirrors"[2] are focal points of energy that are activated by a higher source. Currently beings of feminine polarity carry out the work

---

[1] Aurora, Erks and Miz Tli Tlan. The three greater supraphysical planetary centers now active on the Earth. These have the same name as their corresponding intra-terrestrial centers.

[2] Mirrors. Nuclei that constitute a subtle network of communication and transmission of energies, which permeates all manifested life. Certain specific qualities of the aura on all levels of consciousness determine whether or not a nucleus, such as a planet, a civilization, a group or an individual, is a mirror. Directly or indirectly all

of these mirrors. These beings are also aware of the movements of the forces so that, by keeping them under control, the laws may be accurately carried out. Those who work with the mirrors (and at this time there are some incarnated souls being trained for this) are in charge of seeing that no circumstance and no person should obstruct the fulfillment of the laws. They do this for the benefit of other beings and of the universe.

When passing through different planes, energy infuses a certain quality in each of them and radiates its essence by means of the mirrors. As energy descends, the power of its expression gradually decreases. Therefore, each plane of existence corresponds to a specific gradation of this power and receives it according to its own evolution.

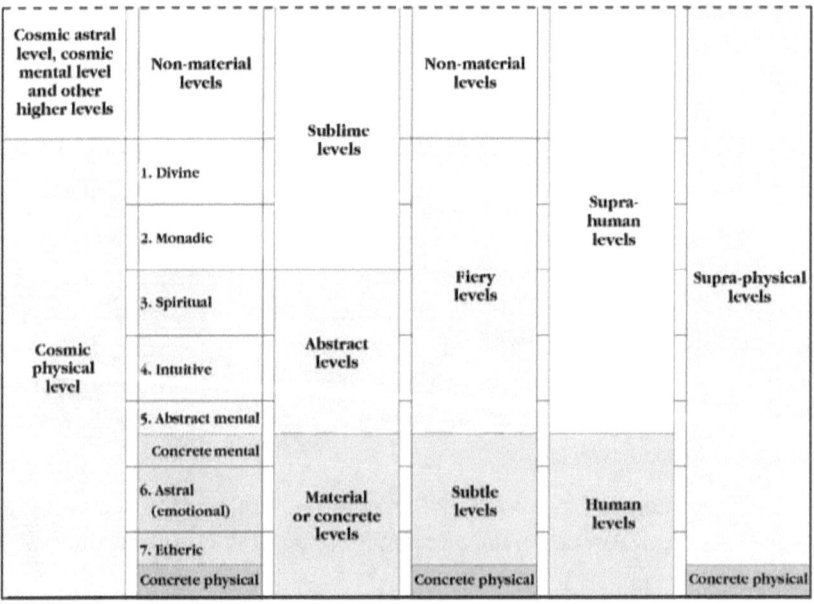

Different ways of looking at the levels of consciousness

beings are in touch with this network of mirrors, but only some are a part of its circuits. The term mirror-being designates souls that are dedicated to this particular work of receiving and reflecting energies in a pure way.

The energy wave that activates the mirrors extends itself. In this way it adapts itself to, and also brings about consequent adaptations in, the beings according to their evolutionary state, thus forming a vast field. This energy field has a broad spectrum but it also serves each individual, for each one receives it according to his or her Hierarchy, task, evolution and corresponding part of the Plan of Evolution.

All energies respond to the mirror systems. Some systems are short-range, while others act more universally. The systems receive energies and transmit them to all that is within their range of action. In this way, through these systems the energies reach the terrestrial plane with the maximum possible potential and they are absorbed according to the level of evolution of the beings who receive them. The energies create a circuitry and communicate through it.

Intraterrestrial civilizations are responsible for the work with the mirrors. In time, this will also be the task of civilizations of the surface as they begin to take on this work. The mirrors are active in the transmission of information, and in the formation of the new race, as well as in the transition of those who wish to come down to this physical plane and fulfill the Law of Service. This does not preclude the work of the Devic Hierarchy in the construction of forms, a work known and disseminated by occultists of all times. The various Hierarchies communicate on different levels, which makes cooperative activities possible. During this phase of the Earth, however, the devas are more dedicated to the mineral, plant and animal kingdoms, and specifically to water in all forms. The work of stimulating and supporting the evolution of the civilizations of the human kingdom is delegated mainly to the monads and the spiritual Hierarchies.

When energy is emitted in its original state of purity for the purpose of reaching a specific plane of existence, the mirrors absorb the power that is expended, eliminated or discharged during its trajectory. The circulating energy is continually worked on and restored to its original state. In this way, because of this perpetual renewal, the energy is able to reach the level of destination fully charged.

As we can see, the work of the mirrors is extremely important for the transmutation of the planetary energies. When the wave of pure energy reaches the terrestrial plane, it immediately transforms the charge emitted by this plane, a charge which is negative due to the atomic residue present there. The activity of the mirrors becomes unified with this transformed positive polarization in transmitting the renewed charge to the future race of the surface.

Everything is generated and emitted by the energies. The mirrors give matter-body the vibratory element that corresponds to its attunement. When combined with the body itself, this vibratory element produces the wave needed by the being. The vibrations of the energies govern all aspects of nature, from the beginning of the first cell of an embryo to the completion of its development. Not for an instant do these vibrations cease being produced. They reach the matter-body through the mirror-wave. The more advanced the being, the greater is the level of his or her vibration, assimilation and information.

There are beings who have achieved the same level of evolution as the ones we call "archangels," yet they descend to the more material planes. When doing this, they must divest themselves of certain energy charges, for their vibration is so intense that the terrestrial human would not be able to withstand their presence without having been prepared. This vibration, comparable in potency to that of a ray, has a very brilliant luminosity that some clairvoyants can see. This luminosity is produced by the friction between that high energy and the atoms of matter, which also evolve as the energies pass through them. Nicolás, for example, is one of those evolved beings. Once he lived on this planet and now he has returned to carry out a specific mission of bringing the voice of the extraterrestrial Hierarchies to the humans of the surface. Nicolás is capable of taking on human form at will. Currently he is in Aurora, which is one of the greater mirrors of South America.

The energy waves emitted by evolved beings such as Nicolás are permeated with vibrations of the fluidic worlds and their radiation can be transmitted to the other worlds. However, those who are on very high planes can only partially descend to the terrestrial planes because the imprint of their reflection on the material world is too strong. The transmission of energy that emanates from them, that is, their communication with the terrestrial levels, is carried out in space with the help of individuals from different planes, including the physical, who are ready for the task. It is through this task, which is one aspect of the broad work performed by the mirrors, that some individuals are prepared for service.

The creator-energies intervene in everything that takes place in such a circuit of transmission, as well as in the circuits where they polarize the energies of those individuals preparing for service and of their worlds. But in order for a creative vibratory circuit such as this to become possible, it is necessary for the mental atoms of the right side consciousness[3] of individuals to become activated. This circuit emerges out of the combination of the creator-energies and energies emitted by the mind.

The merging of the creator-energies with those emanated by the mental world of the planet also has an impact on the atmospheric phenomena controlled by the devas. To bring about these phenomena requires an integration of all those mental waves.

It is not possible for human beings to cooperate with this work without having an understanding of the vibratory waves of the mirrors. One must have the necessary knowledge in order to channel them. For example, in the case of healing, the mental waves begin vibrating, marking out a circuit that is dislodged from the mental body. They enter the space or the atmosphere that surrounds them and there they receive the necessary positive charge of original pure energy. Becoming polarized, they then return to the emitter, causing the sensory centers of the right side of the physical body to vibrate. From there, fully charged, they enter the physical body of the infirm person.

If given the right direction, both cosmic and human energies are able to generate transformations through a powerful action that so far has been ignored by humans from the surface of the Earth. Human beings have an incalculable treasury of knowledge currently hidden in the depths of their own world. The lack of understanding that is characteristic of the superficial levels of human consciousness has caused that treasure to remain buried together with long vanished civilizations. The mirrors were known in the spiritual centers of those ancient

---

[3] Right side consciousness. This refers to the supra-mental aspect of the human being. See chapter: "Awakening of the Right Side Consciousness."

civilizations. If love is present in those who accept responsibilities in silence, the mirrors will impart information far beyond what one could foresee.

There are three great mirrors active in what we here refer to as the southern cone, which actually includes the whole of South America. The first of these mirrors is Miz Tli Tlan, located in the Amazonian jungles of Peru. Miz Tli Tlan, which is now awakening, branches out into the jungles of Brazil and is the greatest mirror of light created on the planet by ono-zone energy. The second mirror is Aurora, in the area of Salto, Uruguay. Like Erks and Miz Tli Tlan, Aurora is an intraterrestrial center, however it is a channel for healing through cosmic energy. The third, Erks, is located in the province of Cordoba, in Argentina. Each of these intraterrestrial centers has a specific task, while at the same time, it is part of a triad.

These mirrors have been known since the creation of planet Earth in order for the races to be able to inhabit it when the planetary Law of Procreation would go into effect. These mirrors remained undisclosed until the end of the period of Shamballa, which has now entered a dormant state. In spite of the fact that their existence was known by all the ancient hermetic schools, only today are they being revealed to the general public because it is only in these times that their activity of helping humanity of the surface has begun to be intensified. This is the hour of need and for this reason the reality of their presence on the planet can be announced more openly.

The mirrors were known in the most ancient civilizations. Some of the work done with them has been documented. For example, the French narrative, À l'ombre des monastères thibétains (In the Shadow of the Tibetan Monasteries), states: "The mirror becomes alluring; in a yellow and gold cloud of scintillating fire, beings pass by, shadows are traced and strange scenes and visions from beyond appear. It seems as if the mirror oscillates under the magic power that impregnates it. It is the sign of the secret societies of Asia, which unifies millions and millions of the yellow race."[4]

---

[4] See Jean Marquès-Rivière, Paris, 1929.

This narrative about Tibet also states that "the ancient one now throws handfuls of aromatic herbs into a great incense burner and uncovers a magic mirror on the altar." This is the Great Asian Mirror, in the world of Shamballa of those times.

Today, however, Miz Tli Tlan has awakened to be the originator of the new race. As happened in the past, when the races left the region that is presently the continent of South America to go to what are now the European and Asian continents, another transfer is taking place. The greater mirror known as Shamballa is beginning a period of dormancy and Miz Tli Tlan is now becoming the significant mirror for the new times.

Since the date of 8/8/88 (August 8, 1988)[5] many have awakened in response to the call to become renewed. The spiritual growth of this world is to take place according to the vast cosmic plan to which this greatest of the mirrors of light is linked. Something harmonious and perfect in human beings will happen when the awakening of their right side consciousness becomes total rather than merely partial. They will feel the call of the three major intraterrestrial centers: Miz Tli Tlan, Aurora, and Erks. They will become aware of this stimulation on their individual being and on their inner life. Their aim will be to reach a new and complete state of consciousness based on the dynamic perfection of the being, a state that will be more consonant with what humans are intended to manifest.

Presently, there is a call coming from different constellations, directed by the Hierarchies that are present on this planet, for humans to express their rightful cosmic heritage. Human beings are cosmic in their essence. Their reality is transcendent. They are divine beings, capable of living within themselves and of rising above their own world. Despite the appeal of their earthly surroundings and the lure of this world, human beings do still continue to seek their source of creation.

---

[5] 8/8/88 (August 8, 1988). Date that marks the beginning of a new solar cycle and the entrance of the planet into a phase of purification, also called the phase of transition.

This is where the light of the mirrors comes in to help human beings to become integrated with their world as well as with the extraterrestrial dimension, guiding them to go beyond the conditions of the current race of the surface. With the light of the mirrors there will be a more harmonious relationship between what is material and what is nonmaterial, for humans will go on seeking inner perfection and spiritual liberation, all the way to the cosmic world. The cosmic world calls for the return of human beings to its bosom.

But the reality within each one must be based on direct knowledge of divine life. Therefore, growth of spirit is to be the primary concern of the new humans because they must vibrate in harmony with divine life even while interacting with the planet and its material levels. Reality touches individual mental beings through the divinity that they perceive, or try to perceive. They will thus become attuned with the monad or the Logos and will grow in divinity. All this is an inward movement.

The monads work to perfect human beings and their spiritual formation. The Planetary Logos draws them toward a complete change, integrating them with the evolutionary law of the cosmic plane. Cosmic life can be found through integration with the mirrors. Currently the Mirror of the Semi-God, Amuna Khur[6] is awakening. Amuna Khur is there in Miz Tli Tlan, as He was in Shamballa. However, whether in Aurora, Erks or Miz Tli Tlan, the power and the perfection of this divine spirit are always present. The entire process is spiritual and this is why we are expressing it in these terms. The process consists above all in seeking the patterns of the higher worlds and not merely the patterns of Earth. The doors are open. Is this not clear?

Individual work must still be carried out, although human behavior in general is to be guided by the Hierarchies of the Cosmos through the education that will come with the new law that will govern planet Earth. New genes are already free of terrestrial karma. The soul is

---

[6] Amuna Khur. A high consciousness that expresses the Planetary Logos, formerly referred to as Sanat Kumara, the Lord of the World.

cosmic and matter is terrestrial; mind and life are powers of the being and these powers can either be developed or left undeveloped.

In Miz Tli Tlan a process of development controlled by the universal mind and carried out by Amuna Khur will make it possible for humans to express the inner sense of the soul. Mind and life alone cannot bring about this process. The new human beings can help the growth of their inner self by projecting a mental attunement upon it, acquired through the stimulating rays of the mirrors, or rather, of the greater mirror that controls the feminine light of creation, and determines the influence of the energies on human beings.

Human beings are predestined to grow in this way. Aided in their self-development, they will harmoniously bring forces under control. A sense of religiousness of the embodied spirit is the expression of the new child of light and of the cosmic universe. The embodiment of the supra-conscious mind is an emerging tendency. This does not take place through what is already known within the boundaries of current thought, but through evolutionary essence, through self-knowledge.

When this phase is completed the present structure of the inner self will have changed and the feminine aspect will be the source of the new creator-action. The task now is to enter into the new rhythm within one's own self. This is the condition that the Supreme Being is presenting to humanity today. Philosophy lives within. Once they perceive this, humans begin to create from their own cosmic level. Their lives and their more subtle bodies are then instruments that will become integrated with the new world, a world that will be born at the end of these times.

This entire process begins when human beings discover the thread of light that connects them with their spirit and when they become devoted to their inner Self. There can be no divinization of external existence if there is no divinization (or progress) of the inner Self. Although veiled, divinity exists in the spiritual core of humans. When they perceive that the aim of nature is to exist in cosmic fullness, this also becomes their only goal.

Without surrender, the total transformation of the current basic structures will not occur. The new Law of Mutation is the light of the mirrors. The call is there, and the decision made by human beings is the work of the Will that claims them as its children. The Will is present, in varying nuances, in each and every individual.

The spiritual growth to which we refer goes beyond prayer, or rather beyond the known limitations of prayer. The vessels of the Space Gardeners[7] are already crossing the skies and they symbolize this consciousness that is being formed. The vessels seek to awaken human beings to self-knowledge. Individuals must feel a total delight in being, for without this they continue to be minimized; they have existence but lack the full Light of the Self. This delight is not external, but intrinsic, self-engendering and independent of whatever may be manifested outside of the human being.

We have been given to know of the existence of the three great mirrors, so let us look at each one.

Aurora is a mirror where extraterrestrial civilizations converge and unite with its intraterrestrial civilization. This is carried out in order to fulfill the Divine Plan for the transition of planet Earth. Aurora provides the base from which to carry out the projects in this transition that are unknown to human beings of the race of the surface.

Erks is a mirror that is integrated with Aurora and is composed of an intraterrestrial civilization and of extraterrestrial beings who also come from other galaxies to contribute to the great mission of changing the race of the surface. When necessary, their task includes taking on physical bodies. In order to do this they perform a transmutation, which means that they bring back to life and use a body that has gone through clinical death. They can also use the bodies of those who have already completed their spiritual-evolutionary stage on Earth and who are leaving for more subtle dimensions, in full knowledge that their sheathes will be used as instruments by more evolved entities to fulfill part of the great plan.

The Law of Procreation, which normally governs the process of terrestrial incarnation, is not followed by these beings from Erks because of the short period of time in which the Law of Mutation is to

---

[7] Space Gardeners. Cosmic entities that watch over the evolution of the races in the different worlds.

be applied on planet Earth, and for other reasons as well. In these cases, when a sheath is ready, the being who inhabited it is transmuted to a higher plane. At the same time, one of the higher beings gives up its present state in order to descend to this physical plane, with the intent of assisting the race of the surface to fulfill its evolutionary cycle.[8]

In Miz Tli Tlan, the greatest of the mirrors, certain Hierarchies work with Amuna Khur, directing the missions of Aurora, Erks and other planetary centers and regulating the development of the plan for the transition of planet Earth and of the race of its surface. This action is integrated into the great cosmic plan, which is coordinated by the higher Council of the Central Celestial Government.[9]

The three major planetary centers in the present cycle

---

[8] See Trigueirinho, Signs of Contact. See also, Carol Parrish-Harra, Messengers of Hope [Tahlequah, OK: Sparrow Hawk Press, 2nd Ed., 2001].

[9] Central Celestial Government. One of the names given to the Hierarchical core of the cosmos, from which creation is organized and sustained.

The names of these three great mirrors, which are intraterrestrial cities, have the following meanings. Aurora is the new dawn (the word aurora in Portuguese and Spanish means dawn), the new day, a stage that is now beginning in order to bring about the transformation of the Earth. Erks is the acronym[10] for "the gathering of sidereal cosmic remnants" ("Encontro de Remanescentes Kósmicos Siderais"). The word "remnant" refers to the brothers and sisters who have come from different points of the universe and who are carrying out their task here in the environs of the Earth to further cosmic fulfillment and unity. Miz Tli Tlan means "the wise ones," source of knowledge and wisdom, the greater light for the spiritual cosmic integration of human beings.

These centers take part in the task of establishing the new race on the surface of this planet, a work undertaken by the universal cosmic being. Sri Aurobindo[11] emphasized that to discover the Divine, as consciousness, is the highest reason for seeking truth and spiritual life. Like all teachers of humanity, he affirmed that this quest is the one indispensable thing and that without it, all else is meaningless.

---

[10] Although Erks is an acronym it is written like a proper name.

[11] Sri Aurobindo. An instructor from India who endowed humanity with new light on the coming stages of evolution of the human species.

Presences That Make Themselves Known

Excerpted from: Mirna Jad—Inner Sanctuary,
by Trigueirinho

When one's aura is attuned and in harmony with the Commands,[1] contacts with intra or extra-terrestrial supraphysical reality take place no matter where one may be. This is because these contacts come from one's inner world and emerge into consciousness, like daylight filtering through slats in the blinds.

Certain areas on the physical plane of the Earth, however, have a specific role and their magnetic field can be organized in such a way that these contacts may more easily take place. These areas are important for the preparation of groups for the planetary rescue,[2] and for the work to support the transition.[3]

---

[1] Commands. Spiritual Hierarchies, great consciousnesses in charge of giving impulse to the Plan of Evolution on Earth. They predominantly express the divine energy of Will.

[2] Planetary rescue. The transfer of life and beings from all kingdoms of nature according to the laws of evolution in the present phase of the transition of the Earth. The beings who cannot follow the new rhythm of the evolution of the Earth will be transferred to other planets. Those who can follow this evolution are being inwardly stimulated and prepared for a new life on Earth.

[3] Transition. The current purification phase of the change of cycle on Earth, and the preparation to enter a new era.

Nowadays humans are receiving great help as they seek to become fully open to these contacts.

One day, as we started out along the country lane that led to an area where contacts would take place, we became aware of the movement of opposing forces. On the subtle planes, those forces circulate on the fringes of evolutionary works, waiting for some door to open for them to slink in and do their work of disintegrating. They are not interested in any specific individual but rather in taking over some human vehicle in order to sow the seeds of chaos. That day the forces were noticeably there, but the energy of a Higher Presence prevailed.

During that gathering to align our bodies[4] for prayer and inner commitment, several of us were aware of a special slightly sweet aroma that pervaded the group. It drew us more and more inward. We knew that such outward manifestations do not happen for us to become attached to them. They adjust our aura and our vibratory field and raise our being to a plane where inner work may take place. We always kept before us the need to have foremost in our minds the true Goal, that is, nonmaterial life and not what our senses experience.

We formed a circle. There were twenty one of us on the physical plane. It was a cloudless night and we could clearly see some space vessels among the stars and planets. We chanted some mantras that helped to prepare the magnetic field for the contact.

Certain things are very mysterious to human consciousness because of the limited inner development of humans and the physical laws which rule the material planes where they exist on the surface of the Earth. Accustomed to being guided by their outer senses, people sometimes allow themselves to become misguided and do not look beyond. During that gathering something very unique was taking place, even though not everyone noticed it. While we were going home some of us were very aware of how we had been worked on by the inner energies that night. An aroma also accompanied us as we returned, while an almost tangible Presence filled our beings. It seemed to be preparing us for broader contacts in the future.

---

[4] Align our bodies. This refers to the integration of the physical-etheric, emotional and mental bodies with the soul or with an even deeper nucleus of the being.

We realized that nothing more should keep us away from the Goal. The help we needed to move ahead was available to us, as an opportunity that comes cyclically. We had to continue to be totally surrendered to the energies and to be detached so that we could express inner life with the necessary humility.

Some days later during a meeting dedicated to inner work on a subtle level, I saw the floor of the room where we were, open up. It seemed as though it had been torn, uncovering a direct entrance to the inner world. A passageway descended vertically to the inner part of the Earth. It appeared to have been built a long time ago but only then was it being revealed. The veil that separated us from it on the etheric planes had been parted. The presence of the group gathered there and the work we had done with the mantras had contributed to making this possible.

A very strong energy came up through that passageway and flooded my being with gratitude and silence. We could feel a connection between the inner world and the cosmos, for that energy expanded into the infinite, while the house and the group acted as intermediaries.

The experience continued when I opened my eyes. The perception of inner reality overshadowed the physical world. I continued to see that passageway open in the floor from where a blessed energy was flowing. I then had the impression that the passageway would not only be accessible during those moments but that it would remain open.

We continued to get together as a group, always placing ourselves at the service of the Plan of Evolution. We learned that it was necessary to keep a balance among the participants of the meetings so that the right persons would be present and the valuable energy available would not be wasted. Once, during a silent group meeting we felt as if we had been drawn into the Alpha Space Vessel.[5] This inner experience was happening on a nonmaterial level. The group was within an

---

[5] Alpha Space Vessel. An important supraphysical cosmic base rendering service to the Earth. It works in the field of inner healing as a preparation for future stages of the development of the human kingdom and of the planet as a whole. It expresses a state of consciousness that is on a galactic level.

energy sphere, which was its own aura, and at the same time inside the energy of the Alpha Space Vessel. Omnipresent, this energy was inside and outside the group and could be perceived as a very clear and "silent" light. We then recited the Sohin[6] mantra[7] and opened ourselves to the energy of the Alpha Space Vessel.

Once we became aware of the non-physical reality that permeated us, the vibration became more intense. It was as though the work were being carried out on various levels of consciousness, taking on a different form at each level. There was a great need for the group to meet in prayer this way. A sense of devotion and of surrender was being nurtured while our outer bodies and psychic aura were being purified. The action of the energies was tangible.

Some more experienced fellow beings from extraterrestrial and intraterrestrial worlds are in charge of preparing the bodies of those humans who are to be evacuated during the rescue operation. These are not the Greater Hierarchies, but channels for their action. In this way our bodies, receptive to the inner contact, were being prepared.

Through these experiences, I was also made aware of something significant for our group work: certain areas where we used to go led us to knowledge of the inner world, while other areas brought the intraterrestrial world up to the surface, thus completing a cycle.

ೋ

Contact between humans from the surface of the Earth and intraterrestrial civilizations has been cultivated since Antiquity. This contact has been the privilege of a few because dense forces of involution

---

[6] Sohin. Cosmic Hierarchy of healing, regent of the work carried out by the Alpha Space Vessel.

[7] Sohin Mantra. Sohin / Sohin / Sohin / Sohin / Manuak Sikiuk Nagua / Manuak Sikiuk Nagua — Pronounced: sō ēn / sō ēn / sō ēn / sō ēn / mä nōō āk sē kē ōōk nä wä / mä nōō āk sē kē ōōk nä wä — Key to symbols: ōō as in boot, ē as in bee, ō as in toe, ä as in father.

wandering the Earth did not allow it to happen on a wider scale. Those who dedicated themselves to inner life in the old monasteries knew a great deal about the existence of these civilizations. However, since they practiced a vow of silence, their experiences were only revealed to their teachers.

What we understand to be God's ways are also humanity's ways when they are followed in fulfillment of Universal Law. We can recognize these ways when we are imbued with that Law.

Intraterrestrial civilizations have always sent healing energy and vibrations of equilibrium to the surface of the Earth and now our link with them is being revitalized. Our Being can contact its cosmic essence in the inner sanctuary of Mirna Jad.[8]

Many Hierarchies are present in the heart of Mirna Jad. Certain patterns of vibration that emanate from the Great Central Council of Miz Tli Tlan imprint the designs of the Most High on the ethers as they become incorporated on each plane of the civilization of Mirna Jad.

A subtle system of short range mirrors interconnects several sublevels of the civilization of Mirna Jad. The activities of those mirrors is accompanied by a vibration of praise.

Intraterrestrial brothers are more and more frequently drawing near our material bodies. As has been announced, once again the Great Brotherhood will be in the midst of humanity of the surface. The pathway goes on being prepared whenever we open ourselves to these contacts. It is as though an eternal and blessed Presence were being glimpsed, if only for brief moments. Part of our group work is to nurture these contacts so that awareness of this reality may endure, nevermore to vanish.

---

[8] Mirna Jad. One of the seven main planetary centers. It synthesizes the energy of the three greater planetary centers, Miz Tli Tlan, Aurora and Erks, and transmits this energy to humanity of the surface. It is a direct extension of Miz Tli Tlan.

The Transfer of Planetary Energies

Excerpted from: Mirna Jad—Inner Sanctuary,
by Trigueirinho

Ancient energy centers of the Earth are being deactivated and their energies are being transferred to other regions of the planet. This, and other changes in the planetary body, are attempting to bring about the all-round balance that has to be attained during a given phase of the Earth's evolution. Therefore, we must let go of nationalism and not be confined to the boundaries or to previous phases of spiritual teaching. We must transcend both external reality and traditions.

One intraterrestrial realm can withdraw from activity, as in the case of Shamballa, while another can enter into activity, as in the case of Miz Tli Tlan. The departing one continues to exist and remains on its own level, but its light is no longer being manifested. Therefore it does not participate directly in the interaction process of the various spheres of consciousness of the planet. On the other hand, the one that enters into activity becomes lighted up. This light then radiates out to all those spheres and interacts with them.

The realm of Mirna Jad is also awakening today, spreading its light throughout the planet and sending out to every corner the essence of life emanating from the Mother-center, Miz Tli Tlan. It is active on the inner planes, where there is no sense of space, but taken from an external point of view, it is situated in South America. Mirna Jad can project itself directly on the surface plane in four different areas of this continent.

Inter-dimensional entrances exist throughout the physical level, regardless of physical and material conditions. At the time of the rescue several intraterrestrial centers will receive a portion of humankind from the surface of the Earth through these centers. Like Mirna Jad, they interact with the centers that fulfill a broader task on the planetary energy circuit.

Intermediate areas between the surface and the intraterrestrial worlds are being prepared to receive human beings who are to be rescued and who will have their subtle bodies worked on before they can enter the intraterrestrial civilizations. In these areas, which are like pockets of energy, they may go into a state of dormancy, assisted by those beings of the surface who were rescued previously and have been prepared for this task, as well as by their intraterrestrial fellow beings. Part of this work is already being carried out today, some of which takes place in space vessels. Nevertheless, during the massive rescue operation, many subtle bodies, scarred by their experiences on the outer planes, will need an intermediate field of vibration for their transfer to occur harmoniously.

Even knowing all this, one should always take into account that the Hierarchies in charge of the tasks are continually revising the plans for the planetary evacuation.

In regard to these inter-dimensional entrances, one day I noticed a type of very large chamber, on a dimension close to the physical plane, in the basement of the place where we used to meet. Several beings were working in this apparently oval-shaped space. Because it was something that appeared to be so concrete, I asked my Inner Self for confirmation on the veracity of that impression. The perception continued to be present and after a while it seemed as if I myself were inside the chamber although my dense physical body remained on the surface.

The day before, while we were trying to pick up the correct wording of a new mantra, I had the feeling that we were in a special part of that area. A subtle "door" opened up in the floor, leading to the inner world. Some hours later we perceived something similar while we worked with the same mantra. Once again we felt as if we were in that place but this time we had already established a link with it.

I knew at the time that something from another dimension was being experienced inwardly and it was being received by my conscious self through these impressions. But in the contact with that chamber it was different. The reality that was being revealed was physical even though it was more subtle than the physical sphere of the surface. I was in contact with an intermediate place between the world of the surface and the intraterrestrial strata where great civilizations live their cycles of evolution.

There is a process of elevation of consciousness to go from human to cosmic evolution that develops through different levels which are transcended during the unfolding of the consciousness. This process is carried out through inner work and surrender of the self to the higher Sources of Life.

൭൫

The mental state of humanity of the surface is very different from the intraterrestrial one. In Mirna Jad and in other planetary centers mental energy is perfectly integrated with the transformative activity of ono-zone. Since these centers have a crystalline connection with the higher planes, this mental energy has become a working instrument for them. The goal sought and the task to be fulfilled are recognized as soon as the impulses sent to them emanate from the Main Council. This is similar to what happens in a healthy organism in which life energy reaches all the cells with the intensity and quality that are appropriate for their functioning.

Since the Realm of Mirna Jad is governed by laws that are higher than the ones we know, there is no struggle for life nor is there a sense of time such as we know it. The succession of events is perceived in a different way on each plane and consciousnesses move from one plane to another, according to the need of the whole Realm. When these consciousnesses contact inhabitants of the terrestrial sphere to take instruction or healing to them the auras and the bodies of the intraterrestrial beings must undergo continual rebalancing.

Even when human bodies from the surface are within the intraterrestrial aura, they continue to be governed by the Law of Disintegration of Matter. Until the new genetic[1] code is fully implanted in them, they can only remain in Mirna Jad for certain periods of time. The healing work carried out there makes it possible for molecules to respond to the new genetic code that is being incorporated by those who, on the surface, are embodying their real identity as Children of the Sun.

The Realm of Mirna Jad, Realm of Eternal Light, extends its radiance to humans of the surface who are pure of heart and who can receive into themselves the rays of a new dawn.

---

[1] New genetic code. A mutation that is taking place in the human species, beginning at the supraphysical levels. See chapter: "The New Genetic Code."

The Current Role of Lis-Fatima

Excerpted from: The Resurgence of Fatima —Lis, by Trigueirinho

The energy of the intraterrestrial center of Lis[1] reaches out in a circle that encompasses the Iberian Peninsula and other parts of Europe. France is among the places magnetically influenced by Lis, and the work that has been done in Lourdes[2] is also fruit of its radiation.

In France, the energy of Lis had a penetrating effect on humanity during the time of the monarchy, and for this reason the fleur-de-lis was used as a symbol of the royalty of that country. It also has esoteric meanings.

Lis is not limited just to Fatima.[3] As a vibratory level, Lis goes deeper than intraterrestrial Fatima. Fatima could be understood as a vestment of this deeper nucleus.

Lis-Fatima also participates in the melding of the races, in the occult rather than the physical-genetic sense of the term. One of the tasks of this center is to inwardly stimulate the formation of etheric patterns that are used to mold the configuration of the sheath of the New

---

[1] Lis. One of the seven principal planetary centers that are active at this time. This center prepares humanity to transcend earthly ways, seeking higher fulfillment.

[2] Lourdes. A place in France known worldwide for the apparitions of the Virgin.

[3] Fatima. A city in Portugal, one of the places where the projection of the planetary center of Lis occurred.

Human. Therefore, it is working toward the formation and emergence of the Fifth Race.[4]

Whenever the inner connection with Lis-Fatima emerges in my being, a state of peace and purity comes over me, represented by a certain lake in Portugal. However, when attunement with another plane of that same center takes place, the impression is different, for an intense and rapid movement of energy is felt, a movement that has within itself profound order, a basis for future manifestations.

There are places on the surface of the planet that maintain a direct energy relationship with this center of Lis-Fatima. However, there is no intention here of stimulating pilgrimages to sacred places. This would be a mere repetition of what has already happened in humanity's past that contributed to retarding its evolution. Those who, on the physical plane truly need to arrive at some area connected with one of the intraterrestrial centers will certainly be led there.

Fatima is a nucleus for transmutation of matter. As the more external counterpart of Lis, it acts on material strata, with the aim of furnishing each atom, cell or being with the redimensioning of energy needed to incorporate the new archetypal pattern that will be expressed there.

A mature relationship between humanity and the essential truth of those intraterrestrial centers is currently impossible and this is one of the reasons for the dynamic action of the Law of Purification. Evolution takes place through successive layers. Although material life is far from expressing the Plan foreseen for it, the cycles of existence on purer levels of consciousness must be fulfilled.

Imbued with this energy, on the inner planes I saw a lot of explosions occurring on the surface of the Earth, one after another. In that vision, war among nations was already a reality. A voiceless voice

---

[4] Fifth Race. According to Theosophy, the Races are vast cycles of the evolution of humanity in which certain formerly latent attributes of the human being are developed. Each race has seven subdivisions. We are currently in the fifth sub-race of the Fifth Race. A Race is fully developed in the sub-race with the same number as the race.

resounded in my inner ears on a plane that was very close to the subtle-physical one:

> Hunger, poverty and corruption will devour one another. What was created by humans to kill fellow humans will turn on those who created it. The face of this planet will be ever more desolate with the unfolding of the final moments of this cycle.

Lis-Fatima represents the Creator-Essence in its expression closest to humankind and brings the necessary knowledge for key moments of the current transition. When this kind of revelation is given to an individual, it remains imprinted in the ether of the planet and can become a warning for all others. And so the revelations continued occurring within me. I saw hordes of starving people running madly along the streets. Fire and plunder were commonplace in the life of the cities.

Humanity does not have the elements or the inner knowledge to allow it to free the planet from the yoke of the forces of involution and it should not confront these forces. It is up to humans to surrender to the Supreme Reality and in total submission, to give their life up to the Life of the Spirit. Thus they can contact the cosmic energies that are currently working for the liberation of the Earth. Only in this way will the Purpose, which silently awaits the dawning of the New Day, be revealed.

Fatima, as a center, announces the great dawn and draws close to human consciousness, summoning the servers to be committed, through their lives, to what the spirit has already fulfilled on its own level.

To the individuals who worry about what may happen to their own physical body, Fatima reveals that this is no longer the time to look for safe geographical areas. One must be like a lone hermit who, having found inner peace, will be led to the correct place even amidst widespread external chaos.

When people sincerely aspire to be attuned to the Universal Law, they no longer depend on external circumstances to feel protected. According to the Gospels, the Son of Man had nowhere to lay His head,[5]

---

[5] See Luke 9:58.

and He attained higher initiations. Even though they may not be totally aware of it, rescuable beings do have will, surrender and determination established within them. These will emerge at the necessary moments, allowing true service to take place. Therefore, any worrying about future days is useless.

♋

One night, during vigil with a group, the energies of both Fatima and Lourdes became even more present. However, the difference between one and the other was evident. In a certain way Fatima brought guilelessness and expressed receptivity, lightness and virginity, whereas Lourdes transmitted a more mature consciousness to us. Lourdes had a task that was instructive rather than constructive, and currently it expresses less potency than Fatima.

The energy of Lis, like the energy of all intraterrestrial centers, varies in intensity during the course of the planetary cycles. Therefore, when one expression comes through stronger than another, it is due to the gradation of the energies that are needed at that specific planetary moment.

When the Hierarchies and the Great Beings who work preparing humanity for the new cycle and for the planetary transition need to reach humanity's consciousness, they have to use whatever material that is available on the conscious and subconscious mental plane of humanity of the surface.

The figure of the Virgin is a very old symbol and continues to be powerful, thus it can best translate the vibratory quality, the tone and the purity of the energy of the two centers. This symbol has been used as a means to contact the consciousness of terrestrial humans.

Every symbol has within it the keys to past, present and future stages. Even if it is eventually substituted by a symbol that would better channel or synthesize the note to be sounded in a certain phase, its essence remains unalterable because it already existed before the creation of the Worlds.

If we had to speak of something transcendental to a child we would certainly express ourselves through images and symbolic illustrations. In the same way, humanity is still a child and also has to be awakened by means of symbols, to the cosmic reality that is becoming established on this planet.

The purpose of the so-called appearances of the Virgin, which are projections carried out by the extraterrestrial or intraterrestrial vessels, is to stimulate devotion in human beings at the present cyclical time and, as a consequence, to strengthen their link with spiritual levels. Once this is done, people should no longer need the form that led them to that point because they would have been touched by the essence. However, this is not what has happened with humanity of the surface. This humanity is still crystallized within the conditions of a civilization that opted for material values in detriment to expansion toward the life of the spirit. Humanity became attached to formalities and thus lost the true sense of what was being disclosed. Naive persons gave in to the inertia of emotional prayers and formal petitions for healing, leaving the celestial sources to take on what they should have accomplished in themselves through their own efforts.

The energy manifested by a spiritual center in a given phase is only one of the many facets of its magnanimous presence. If humanity does not take into itself the essence of such manifestation and use it as a step leading toward liberated Life, it will not receive the grace that emanates from the following level. As each opportunity is rejected, humans distance themselves in consciousness from the possibility of glimpsing wider horizons.

However, the day will come when Celestial Light will permeate the light within matter and then this Earth will truly know the energy of the winged kingdoms. No longer will chaos and discord or degradation emerge from a life separated from the Supreme Purpose. The archetypes will take shape and the atmosphere of the Earth will welcome the sacred flight of the spirit.

Humanity will then contemplate stellar horizons and will know the promise that was made to it. Humans will respond wholeheartedly to the commands of the Greater Light that summons them. They will know how to recognize their true task and will accomplish it as part of their own essential being. This promise is safeguarded in Lis-Fatima, which shelters within its pristine core the purity of the coming times.

Incubation or Sleep in the Temple

Excerpted from: Aurora —Cosmic Essence of Healing,
by Trigueirinho

There is a link between health and energy. A pure life prepares the human being to contact higher energies. Therefore one's life should be the reflection of one's convictions and not something that runs parallel to what one believes but never puts into practice. Vices lead to the breakdown of the nervous substance.

It is important not to concentrate too much attention on one's physical body. One should focus on the Most High, not on the bodies He has created. However, it is crucial to do this in a balanced way so that one may progressively attain synthesis.

From now on human beings will have their innate intellectual capacity increased through the new genetic code[1] and will no longer single out material aspects from the others. The merging of practical science with spiritual philosophy will have been reached on planet Earth. No study of human beings can be separated from the universe

---

[1] New genetic code. Laws that govern the transformation currently underway in the human species, which will allow for greater contact with nonmaterial worlds. See chapter: "The New Genetic Code."

where they exist. All fields of science are interdependent and everything should be viewed as a whole and not in a fragmented way.

Physical science, social science and spiritual science are in fact one, even though our civilization has regarded them as independent fields. When there is no spiritual knowledge of man and of the cosmos, physical science gets lost in conflicts with natural laws. Nowadays social science is limited to being no more than an instrument of political and economic forces and it cannot really exist without the other two sciences. As for spiritual science, it is little studied these days. However, we must bear in mind that a planet that does not take spiritual science into account is alienated from the life of the solar system and of the galaxy where it exists. Nowadays terrestrial physical science and social science are typical of the planetary laws that rule the material-physical plane. If these branches of science do not relate to the domain of spiritual science, they will remain severed from their origins and far removed from their overall goals and the cosmic laws that should govern them.

The present chaos will be resolved through the Law of Purification. In his aphorisms, Hippocrates presented some indications for the proper functioning of the physical body. Although he seemed to be referring only to the physical plane, he was in fact alluding to material aspects of supraphysical laws. For example, he said: "If a body is in pain, this means that it was attacked by illness; but if those who are ill do not feel pain, then illness attacks the spirit." Hence, the Law of Purification may bring pain to the sick person. This Law, which will transform the Earth by means of cataclysms and a process of selection, is pure Love, even though it may be incomprehensible in the three lower dimensions, that is, the mental, emotional and physical.

Although it was known in the past that there is no substantial difference between medicine and philosophy, this knowledge has been lost in today's medical practice. Medicine is philosophy when it seeks the causes of illness, the inner causes, on different depths. People who do not have this perspective and live superficially without attuning to other planes of existence, cannot practice true medicine because they are not able to understand such things as the kind of illness that simply disappears without any apparent treatment.

An ancient text states: "Your fees will be of no use to you except to develop and improve your art; they are to be adjusted according to the means of your clients. You will first attend to the strangers and the poor, supplying what they need, not only with treatment but also with money." This was the norm for doctors in the past. These principles have been forgotten by most, but not by all.

ॐ

In Greece, four centuries before Christ, Aesculapius performed cosmic healing. In time this healing became the practice of medicine as it is known today. During this innovative work, the sick would go to any of the four hundred temples of Aesculapius and would be cured during their sleep through what was known as incubation or sleep in the temple. Upon arrival, the sick persons would make an offering of themselves to the gods and would purify themselves by means of baths, abstinence and diets. Then they would go to sleep in a kind of shelter that was open on all sides so that the fresh air could circulate freely.

During the night, Aesculapius would come to the person in dreams and provide the necessary guidance. In some cases, patients would be submitted to surgery during a dream and when they awoke in the morning they would find that they had been cured. In this shelter, which was the temple, patients often sensed that a ray of energy descended and sometimes touched their sick bodies while they were fast asleep. These perceptions would come from other planes and not from their outer senses, which at the time were probably sleeping along with the physical body.

The vision the patients might have of Aesculapius during their sleep was a revelation and in some cases, they would even hear his voice. These methods were also known at the Oracle of Delphi where, according to the history of medicine, certain forms of psychotherapy suitable to those times were practiced. These psychotherapies had their roots in the cosmic essence of healing and were not delimited by a rational content.

In Aurora the practice of incubation takes place in a way similar to that of the temples of Aesculapius, but with its own characteristics. It is a completely inner process. Therefore, today cosmic healing has returned in a new light. While in ancient times the process of healing in the temple was conducted by Aesculapius from supraphysical levels, now this work is inspired by cosmic beings who are active in other civilizations or on other levels.

The beings from Aurora work without the limitations of space or time. To illustrate this, I would like to describe what happened to someone who had cancer and was traveling to North America to undergo tests. Before departing, this person had sought inner contact with the energy of one of the healers from the intraterrestrial center of Aurora, asking for help. This healer was Padre Pio.[2] Upon arriving in the US, the tests were carried out and the results were negative. The doctors, who knew about the clinical condition of the patient, looked for an explanation. It was impossible to medically account for what had happened. However, something significant had occurred on the physical level that had left evidence. During the flight this person had photographed the clouds. Upon arriving, the film was developed and the person noticed that an image could be seen in the midst of the clouds. The image was that of the being to whom she had appealed for help. It was formed of clouds and a black spot could be seen in the place that corresponded to the area in her body affected by cancer.

Thus healing again takes on higher cosmic aspects on the Earth. . Payment for services is typically terrestrial and therefore can only be applied when the treatment is based on accepted material laws.

The meaning of cosmic healing is not limited to physical laws of this planet, laws that have dense vibration. The only requirement for healing in the recently restored process of incubation or sleep in the temple, is faith. "Do you have faith?" Christ would ask the sick. When the answer was affirmative, this authentic cosmic healer, who was never paid for his mission, could then bring forth healing. If the answer were

---

[2] Padre Pio (1887-1968). A Catholic priest who was born in Pietrelcina, Italy, and well known as a healer.

negative or if there were any doubt, nothing could take place, even though Christ himself was the intermediary.

In the temples of Aesculapius the healing ray was regarded as energy controlled by the cosmos. In Aurora, space vessels acting as intermediaries of the cosmos bring this healing energy. As in ancient Greece, there is a mystery in these facts. They are not obscure in themselves, but the still limited human intellect cannot grasp them. Even though medicine today also resorts to sleep as one of its therapeutic techniques and indicates sleep for certain pathologies, this should not be considered the same as the above described incubation. In modern medical practice, sleep is usually induced artificially and cannot always count on the presence of the energy of faith. In cosmic healing, as we have seen, faith is indispensable because it is the thread that links the infirm person's consciousness to the higher nucleus of his or her being. One's higher nucleus is never ill because it transcends the levels where illness exists.

The planetary center of Aurora has been established by sidereal healers who are not incarnate. Brill[3] energy is fundamental for the work of these healers at this time. The methods used by Aesculapius were mystical and supernatural since they worked with the human mind of those days, which was less developed than it is now. In ancient Greece, baths, diets and exercises were used in the field of physical therapeutics. These techniques continue to be valid. However, nowadays we lack the facilities where these techniques could be practiced without having to depend on profits and commercial interests.

In some cases more than one night was needed for cosmic healing in the temples of Aesculapius. At times, patients would go through a process lasting several days or weeks. This can also take place in the new phase of cosmic healing on this planet. This reactivation of healing signals the advent of the new humanity, which will develop having a new genetic code that excludes aggressiveness and attachment to the denser things of the material plane.

---

[3] Brill. One of the extensions of ono-zone energy. Among other uses, the intraterrestrial civilizations apply brill in the healing and regeneration of the bodies.

We are approaching events with deep spiritual repercussions. The increasing chaos in the three dimensional world is part of this play of forces. It will prepare the way for the separation of the wheat from the chaff, so that harmony may be restored to humanity of the surface and to the Earth itself. Other patterns of behavior and other planetary laws will then go into effect.

This transition is controlled by cosmic energies. Despite the visible degenerative processes present today, the higher goal of the future human race will become clear.

Radiation and Healing

Excerpted from: Aurora —Cosmic Essence of Healing, by Trigueirinho.

Healing consists of receiving the energies that emanate from the higher levels of life or subtle worlds. Receiving these energies is the result of one's expansion of consciousness. However, this does not mean that the physical brain will necessarily register such an expansion, even though this would be desirable, and in certain cases could even be presented as a task to be fulfilled.

Whether they are aware of it or not, whether they agree with it or not, in a healing process people should be regarded as a whole, including all levels of their existence and their interaction with all the energies that affect and permeate them. These energies come from the surrounding environment, from humanity itself or from more advanced beings and more evolved worlds. In brief, one must take into account that each human being participates in the cosmos and is unalterably bound to it.

Those who are currently practicing conventional medicine should engage in the development of their own character and purity of life. They should not confuse their profession with materialism. However, those who are instruments of healing in the spiritual sense are able to transmit the transcendent power of the healing energy. This power is expressed as "radiation." True spiritual healers are those who are already in touch with higher levels of consciousness. They create a magnetic field around themselves that takes in everyone and everything, without distinction. And each one receives the energy of healing according to his or her openness to subtle realities.

The energy used by the healer comes from dimensions of the universe that are free from any kind of contamination, psychic or otherwise. Therefore, it cannot bring with it any harmful element. The atomic structure of these higher levels could be called Light, although it has nothing to do with electric light known on Earth. On those levels there is no reaction, tension or conflict of any kind because the polarities are more balanced. Those elevated levels of Light project their energies to specific areas of the solar system, which are nuclei of radiant life and are precisely the points of origin of various healing centers on Earth. Besides these nuclei, even more potent and physically distant constellations send us their energies. To receive and distribute these energies is part of the task of more powerful centers, such as Aurora, Erks and Miz Tli Tlan.

The formation of cosmic healers is also one of the tasks carried out by Aurora. There are beings in that planetary center today who have lived through terrestrial experiences and have taken certain steps to attain the level where they are now. In the future, the healers on Earth will have a broader role. They will not be limited to healing individuals, but their function will be to radiate harmony to the environment where they live, as well as to relatively distant areas. This will depend on the range of their spiritual wave. In no way does this statement imply any form of mind control or mental transmission of rays.

All cosmic healing builds on the transformation of cellular substance. Thus the healer must live a pure life so that this transformation may take place and that he or she may serve as an instrument for this kind of work. The karma of the planet and of human beings is undergoing great change. Now is the right time to come under different laws of this same universal order. Individuals who allow this concealed transformation to take place within their beings open themselves to energies coming from cosmic space. These energies infuse and purify their cells, and produce both disintegration and radiation simultaneously. According to the great teachers, these two processes are directly interrelated. All potential healers should prepare themselves for these processes.

The cells in a healer's life are constantly being bombarded by neutral sets of atoms, free of karma, coming from the spiritual world. This is how energy is liberated at this level. It produces a beneficial radiation that emanates from the healer. Scientists from the Earth know about a similar phenomenon but they have put it to evil use, such as in atomic explosions. In these explosions, set off by humans, the nucleus of the atom is bombarded by physical neutrons, whereas in the aforementioned spiritual healing the process takes place through groupings of spiritual atoms. Healers should live in such a way that their vehicles may be continually transformed and purified to the maximum so that these transcendent atoms may flow through them.

Cosmic healing will be a generalized practice among all those who have chosen to be in the New Earth, an activity that some may already be carrying out. Competitiveness and separateness cannot be present in the ethics of true healers. In addition, a healer should have already developed the capacity to disregard illusory goals. The quality of a healer's life is indicative of his or her stage of evolution.

ೞ೮

Illness is a consequence of the imperfections engendered in the past as well as in the present. Real preventive treatment lies in seeking to perfect oneself. According to Amhaj,[1] healing through Love is more powerful than any physical blood transfusion.

Spiritual healers can work in different ways, either by using their hands or their eyes, or by radiating the energy of Love at a distance. This latter method is more appropriate for the present times as well as for the future. Love does not need to reach the patient's energy centers directly and it can help the organism in its efforts to attain harmony. The touch of Love is imperceptible.

---

[1] Amhaj. The High Commander of Aurora planetary center. El Morya and Master Morya were well-known expressions of this elevated consciousness.

Love avoids being expressed outwardly except when needed. It acts on the subtle planes, leaving no visible signs. In order to be able to do this, healers must have already learned how to apportion their forces correctly, safeguarding them wisely but without omission. It is important not to waste energy on what is superfluous, not even on thoughts.

A true healer very often acts consciously but there are occasions when his or her ray acts without being intentionally directed. Help from the supraphysical world is ready to flow down, but it must find a channel to receive it. This channel is Love, which establishes all the links between humans and the nonmaterial world.

೫೦

Our understanding of the subtle world is limited by emissions coming from decomposed matter. The foul odor attracts lesser developed dwellers from the lower planes. This is one of the reasons why eating meat hinders the refinement of the material bodies. Putrefaction is not acceptable even in vegetables. Some people do not realize how much harm is caused to their consciousness when they eat food that is in a state of putrefaction.

Ordinary scientists deny many things that could be useful for their research. Their mental prejudice is a great obstacle. We should continually adapt ourselves to expansions of consciousness. In the cosmic universe nothing is repeated; everything is always new. Let us, therefore, get rid of our biases.

If we pay close attention we will see that energy can be perceived on the right side of the organism and that smell is the sense which most readily detects subtle emanations. We can smell aromas when there is some "presence" nearby. But it is Love that refines the sense of smell. When a being from the inner world approaches us, it is Love that bestows the quality of the aroma. Some people sense this while others do not. It all depends on the energy of Love that has been developed.

When the mind gives an order, the nerve centers of the physical body go into action and this elicits effort. But Love emanates without any effort at all. In fact, Love can only go into action when there is no tension. Distance is no obstacle in its trajectory.

Our lifestyle should be coherent with the energy that we activate and manifest through our being. Some of us need to practice more restraint than others. Some should no longer eat any animal products, not even dairy products. We should all be vigilant as to what kind of discipline or lifestyle we need to practice.

The fire of Love has not yet been stirred up in most people. When life is too easy, they become lax. This is so with children as well; one should not give in to their wishes too readily. However, we should not worry but do the best we can and trust, because the overall lines of their path have already been predestined.

One may strive to attain a state of harmony through physical, psychological or inner means. But the inner way does not really require effort for it is actually the radiation of the energy of Love. It is quite rare because most people are more familiar with, and dependent on, physical and psychological aspects. Becoming attached to these aspects of one's being merely produces crude illusions.

Evil can only be remediated with goodness. However, goodness only appears sporadically in most people and because of this they frequently become instruments for the forces of involution. As we know, there are various gradations in the manifestation of goodness. According to Amhaj, really virtuous persons never think they are doing all the good they are capable of doing.

The teachings of Amhaj, a guide from Aurora, affirm that inner fire is more potent than outer, terrestrial fire. This fire exudes through the pores of the skin and builds a protection around the person. The Hierarchy invites us to rejoice in what we have achieved and to aspire to collaborate with interplanetary and intergalactic planes. Thus the future race will not have its consciousness confined to the Earth.

All this is not really complex. Purification brings it all about imperceptibly. New rays are penetrating the planet and are also reaching us. We must go forward in the assurance that we are being helped. Even if this cosmic stream may not be felt on all levels of our being, it is always there, present in everything.

Humanity of the surface must be prepared to contact the subtle worlds, the inner worlds. Certain kinds of information and transformation will be needed in order for this to take place and if we are open we can acquire much knowledge to this effect. However, we must bear in mind that the best manifestations of higher energy are not discernible. So let us value silence.

The New World is here. What must we do to see it? The answer comes: be simple. Christ held children up as an example because the way to real discovery does not lie in the intricacies of intellectuality but in spiritual consciousness that reaches down to the depths of the ocean, always encompassing new spheres. When facing danger we must reaffirm our invulnerability, yet without conflict or defiance. We should unify our energies. We can attain immunity when our aspirations are directed toward spiritual fire.

Our vitality is intensified when subtle energies enter into vibration. So let us knock on the right door.

The Great Magnetic Network

Excerpted from: Oceans Can Hear,
by Trigueirinho

The magnetic network of the planet has various nuclei that activate and purify it. This network is linked in a special way to the intraterrestrial center[1] of Iberah.[2] Its function is to join the magnetic streams of the Earth with those coming from the Sun and sidereal space. Its most active nucleus in this phase is the Bermuda Triangle.

Besides the nuclei of the magnetic network, some intraterrestrial centers pick up, transform and radiate cosmic energy on a planetary level. They are highly developed and they have specific tasks in fulfilling the evolutionary aims of the Earth. These centers include civilizations that inhabit supraphysical planes. Although they remain on the intraterrestrial level during the current cycle, they can have extensions on the surface of the planet.

The main intraterrestrial centers active today are: Anu Tea, Aurora, Erks, Iberah, Lis-Fatima, Mirna Jad and Miz Tli Tlan, which have specific extensions of energy mainly in the Pacific Ocean, Uruguay, Argentina, Iberian Peninsula, Brazil and Peru.

---

[1] Intraterrestrial center. See chapter: "Planetary Centers."

[2] Iberah. An intraterrestrial center active since the primordial times of the manifestation of the Earth. It acts powerfully in the redemption of matter. True alchemical science is safeguarded by this center. Despite the fact that humans do not have direct access to it, they receive its emanations through the other intraterrestrial centers, principally Aurora, which is in charge of making this connection.

The seven main intraterrestrial centers

In some cases it is important to know where the intraterrestrial centers are located and to know their areas of influence, how they interact with the other centers and how they carry out their work to aid evolution. Each center fulfills a certain role. To know this role, even if partially, means to be attuned to the inner groups[3] and to the work of the Hierarchy. It means, therefore, to become integrated into the subtle life of the Earth and the cosmos, a life that unifies all these energy networks and centers.

However, since these intraterrestrial centers are not to be found on physical levels, their geographic projection always corresponds to their activity. The physical regions of the terrestrial globe mentioned

---

[3] Inner groups. A gathering of souls and monads under the same Ray energy. These are really energy centers in the body of humanity. Through them humanity receives its evolutionary impulses. They used to be known as inner level Ashrams.

here are merely points of reference. The action of these subtle nuclei is not limited to those regions nor are they subject to any kind of transformation caused by cataclysms or natural disasters that may occur on the surface of the planet.

The aim of the work of the Hierarchy in the manifested world is to guide the world and the beings who inhabit it toward a vibratory state that is consonant with the purpose of evolution. The goals of the Hierarchy are frequently updated so that inner reality may be adequately expressed at each cycle. Humans are being prepared to become integrated into this work. Today, more than ever, the Teaching has become available on the inner levels, awakening the pulsation of light in the core of human consciousness. This awakening also occurs in terrestrial life as a whole, stimulated directly by the planetary centers and indirectly by the magnetic network. This magnetic network applies laws that help the vibrations of human beings become attuned to the vibrations of the higher worlds.

The Teaching transmitted to humanity takes into account the transition that is underway, as well as the future phase of the planet, and addresses human beings even when it deals with generic issues. The Teaching expands human vision and service to the Plan of Evolution and thereby makes it possible for humans to have access to what formerly was concealed from them. Therefore, the principal function of the Teaching is to expand the consciousness of beings who seek it, thus it is given independently of its immediate practical use.

The energy triangle formed by the intraterrestrial centers of Miz Tli Tlan and Anu Tea and the Niskalkat[4] base has special functions in the preparation of humans for future life and encompasses a vast spectrum of energies. The tasks of this energy triangle include:

- To attune with powerful extra-systemic vibrations—a task carried out through the mirrors of Miz Tli Tlan;

---

[4] Niskalkat. A base for operations on the supraphysical levels of Asia. This base provides important support for the work of inner groups on the subtle planes of the Earth.

- To adjust those vibrations to what life on Earth is able to bear as evolutionary stimulation—a task carried out through the mirrors of Anu Tea;

- To mold the energy patterns on the etheric plane. Human beings must adhere to these so that they can also follow the global transition on the external levels—a task carried out through the mirrors of the subtle Niskalkat base.

As one can see, this interactive relationship is expansive and expresses the kind of balance that is very present in a triangular configuration. Besides the tasks mentioned above, the triad of energy centers is in charge of preparing human beings for contact with unknown energies, such as those that are active in the Bermuda area and in other sites.

The impulse for future life flows from the intraterrestrial centers and the subtle bases in the same way that blood, pumped by the heart, runs through one's veins. Therefore, there is no real progress that does not lead to one of the portals of these centers and bases, custodians of the Earth's relationship with the cosmos. Recognizing their energy within ourselves is the immediate outcome of expansions brought about by a life of service.

While reading Twenty Thousand Leagues under the Sea,[5] every now and then we would enter into a very deep state of relaxation that lasted a few minutes. We would then have short dreams, some of which were enlightening. In one of them we were transferred to the region of the Bermudas and we observed its energy from an inner perspective. We could perceive a powerful force that controlled the material and non-material laws there and could see that this force was coming from another region of the planet in a different dimension.

In this experience we did not perceive any "human life" in the area of the Bermudas, such as the life that exists in the supraphysical, intraterrestrial civilizations that we had contacted before, but rather

---

[5] Jules Verne, Twenty Thousands Leagues under the Sea [New York: Bantam Books, 1962].

there was a sort of effervescence of magnetic and electric fluids. If we were to compare it with what we know, we would say that we were on the inside of a dynamo capable of producing and channeling vast potential.

We were then shown the whole surface of the planet and a point in the area of the Bermudas was highlighted on it. That point rose up to a certain level in space. Countless threads of energy connected to other points spread around the globe were attached to it. Thus we learned that the nuclei, which make up the magnetic network being studied here, are processing centers for powerful energies. These nuclei sustain the vibratory stability of planetary life and help the material world receive the aid that comes from parallel universes.

In this way new aspects of the planetary magnetic network were being revealed to us. This network was shown to be indispensable for the balance of the Earth. We learned, through intuitive channels, that it was related to some material factors, such as:

- the configuration of the oceanic floor, with its mountain ranges and trenches;
- the ocean currents.

In Twenty Thousand Leagues under the Sea, Jules Verne draws our attention to these currents: "They are special currents that can be easily recognized by their temperature and color, and the most remarkable of these is the Gulf Stream. Science has been able to determine the place of five such currents: one in the north Atlantic, a second in the south Atlantic, a third in the north Pacific, a fourth in the south Pacific, and a fifth in the southern Indian Ocean. It seems likely that once upon a time a sixth existed in the northern Indian Ocean, when the Caspian and Aral Seas were united to the great Asian lakes and formed a single expanse of water." [6]

---

[6] Jules Verne, op. cit. page 95.

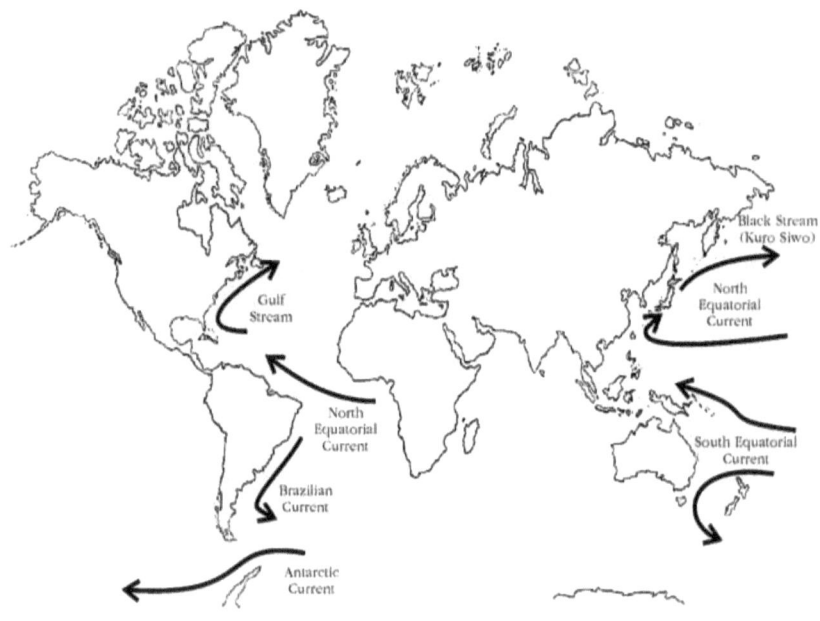

The main ocean currents

Continuing our silent investigation into the annals of the inner world, we saw that one of the tasks of that magnetic network was to disperse the static electricity that is accumulated in the large volumes of ocean water. This work is done steadily but invisibly and so it is very rarely perceived. If it were not for this task, the instability caused by the accumulation of electric energy would probably not allow life to continue on the surface of the Earth.

When we traced the route of the journey of the submarine Nautilus, from Jules Verne's book, on a map, we noticed that it either came close to the energy vortices of the Earth or it actually coincided with them. The circles on the following map correspond to these vortices, most of which have presented observable but unexplainable occurrences.

Energy vortices of the planetary magnetic network

The following vortices, shown on the map above, are part of the planetary magnetic network:

1. North Pole.
2. Bermuda Triangle.
3. Coast of the Iberian Peninsula and of Morocco.
4. Area west of Afghanistan.
5. Devil's Sea (between Japan and the Bonin Islands).
6. Hawaii.
7. Coast of Argentina.
8. Coast of South Africa.
9. Saint Paul, Kerguelen and isolated islands to the south of the Indian Ocean.

10. Tasmanian Sea.

11. Area of intense volcanic activity in the Pacific Ocean, near Pitcairn Island.

12. South Pole.

As mentioned in "A Message From An Earlier Civilization,"[7] the North and South Poles, the Bermuda Triangle, the Tasmanian Sea and the coast of Argentina are part of a network existing under the seas and are outlets for currents of water that emerge from inside the planet. We knew, therefore, that these were passageways to the intraterrestrial world.

Energy-wise, the twelve vortices form this icosahedron

These twelve vortices form the magnetic network that we are studying. However, not all have active supraphysical nuclei. A magnetic vortex is a natural element, a component of the magnetic field of the Earth, whereas a supraphysical magnetic nucleus is created by consciousnesses that guide the evolution of the planet. This creation occurs when a planetary center interacts with the vortex. By analogy, we could say that these supraphysical nuclei are energy processing stations or power plants, while the magnetic vortices are a natural source of the energy with which the power plants work.

---

[7] See page 15.

Some of the magnetic supraphysical nuclei active today[8]

An inner vision made it clear to us how this magnetic network functions. Emphasis was placed on the supraphysical nucleus in the Bermuda Triangle, into which innumerable currents flowed. It seemed to be like the heart of a system that channeled a new, revitalizing energy through various arteries and received material from innumerable veins. This energy was to be selected, processed, expelled and reused. This is one of the functions of the Bermuda Triangle and also of the other components of the magnetic circuits.

Presided over by Iberah, this network acts in conjunction with other intraterrestrial centers, especially Anu Tea and Miz Tli Tlan, as

---

[8] It is no coincidence that in the regions corresponding to the triangles there is always a confluence of marine currents. They change direction at these points. This demonstrates a variation in the magnetic and energy conditions of the surrounding areas.

well as with the intra-oceanic centers. It has a specific role in the planetary body becoming more subtle, as well as in the magnetic relationship of the Earth with the cosmos, and above all, with the Sun and the Moon. In order to help the process of becoming more subtle, this network established a direct contact with an intergalactic base on the Moon and with the Moon itself, for that base uses the lunar magnetism to carry out certain tasks, such as to purify the planet.

The New Genetic Code

Excerpted from: Beyond Karma, by Trigueirinho

The genetic code of a human being is much more than a physical-chemical configuration; it is a set of conditions of energy determined by the archetype for humanity in each evolutionary cycle. It is not limited to the organization of the substances of an organism, nor to its functioning, but it includes its state of consciousness. The genetic code goes beyond the level of matter, and is an instrument for the Plan of Evolution to guide human beings toward the energy pattern they are destined to express.

Since it is a means to bring about the materialization of archetypal patterns and since these patterns are dynamic, whenever necessary a genetic code is modified or substituted by those who govern evolution. Such adjustments are made when human beings move away from the archetypal pattern of a given cycle, or when there is a change in the cycle. In the history of this humanity there have been at least four shifts in the genetic code.

Humanity has reached an impasse in failing to go beyond polarization on the most concrete levels of life. This impasse has been added to what is happening on the Earth, a planet that is to become subtle and to be transferred to an etheric level, free of the present density. This situation calls for profound transformations. Consequently, a more powerful non-material impulse was needed. Thus, a new genetic code, GNA,[1] is beginning to be implanted on supraphysical levels of humanity.

---

[1] GNA. This acronym does not denote a specific chemical substance, but an electromagnetic field.

This planet is becoming progressively more subtle. Therefore, the humanity that will inhabit it will have to have adequate genetic components to be able to express what the planetary consciousness requires as it ascends.

The new genetic code is being introduced into approximately ten percent of human beings, incarnate or not, within the Earth's environs. On the physical plane the bodies will become more subtle; on the spiritual plane this will happen according to the specific laws of that plane.

Until now, hereditary traits, such as height, skin color, physical features, presence or absence of physical defects, as well as some psychological tendencies, have been passed on from parents to offspring through chromosomes. This is precisely what is beginning to change.

For those who are receiving GNA, all this old structure of heredity and karma falls away. GNA is of a stellar and nonmaterial origin. Therefore, under this new genetic code, individuals are not conditioned by the past experiences of their species.

DNA, the genetic code activated in the cycle currently coming to a close, is of animal origin and could only take humanity up to a certain level of evolution. The new genetic code, GNA, is now needed in order to open the way for a greater integration into inner realities.

When human beings still have DNA and are governed by the Law of Karma, their actions on the physical plane create material values and generate either abundance or scarcity, according to the quality of their deeds. Through their feelings humans create values on the level of pleasure and dissatisfaction, thus engendering positive or negative emotional situations, according to the nature of these values. Through their thoughts they create values on the level of ideas, which produce either high ideals and consequent mental health, or pessimism, criticism and disharmony, depending on the quality of their thoughts.

With the new genetic code, human beings will no longer be held captive by their own limited creations. Furthermore, they will lose all aggressiveness and will be able to understand that all goods belong to everyone and not only to a few, and that these goods should be applied in developing spiritual consciousness and not in satisfying egoism.

Because of its origin, GNA gives human beings stability, unity of thought and a sense of fraternity, thus making it possible for them to live consciously on inner levels and within the laws that govern humans. A new vibration is introduced into their subjective world with the implanting of this new genetic code. This vibration is projected from level to level, drawing all the atoms of their bodies into attunement with its frequency, which is subtle and is in accordance with the cosmic goal of their higher self.

In everyday life we should do that which is good, beneficial and useful, detached from any and all fruits of our action, so that we can prepare for the transition from the Law of Karma to the higher Law of Evolution. This teaching is as ancient as the world. But only now, with the implanting of the new genetic code, can the teaching be understood and carried out by a greater number of people. Under the old DNA code even those who seek a spiritual life behave like the Apostle Paul, who declared in one of his epistles that he did not do the good he wanted to do, but did the evil he did not want to do.

However, the forthcoming expansion of consciousness is not based solely on changing the genetic code, or on transcending the Law of Karma. Up until now, only the cells of coarser vibration have been active, especially in the brain, and these cells have had to endure the disorder of human bodies. Nevertheless, a large contingent of cells, destined to pick up and manifest energy waves coming from the spiritual and divine planes, will be awakened.

The awakening of these cells is part of a broad restructuring of this humanity's physical life and depends on the contact that material consciousness has with the soul. This inner contact will bring about a perception that is increasingly freed from egoism and that is less inclined to be linked to people, things and circumstances. In a not too distant future, many people who have a larger portion of active healthy cells will be capable of embracing what is seemingly unpleasant in order to help the evolution of groups and of the planet. They will transcend the level of desire and be able to freely serve the constructor-energies that are performing evolutionary works in the cosmos.

The new genetic code, GNA, can also be developed and manifested on the denser planes of existence whenever people are receptive to what it inspires and stimulates. Those who are not open to transformation may reject the new code, which then withdraws to subjective levels until the nodules of resistance are dissolved. Depending on the degree of reaction contrary to the nonmaterial impulses prompted by GNA, this genetic code may even be canceled and the person may only become integrated into this evolutionary current in a future cycle.

When the new genetic code becomes fully implanted and embodied, human beings will tend to express unity of aspirations and goals on their mental level. GNA draws cosmic patterns of life down to the Earth and builds the foundations for the New Humanity. It predisposes human beings to become more subtle and its vibration opens the doors of consciousness to experiences and to life on higher planes. Through GNA the energy potential of these planes causes matter to become more fluid. This process, in close collaboration with the soul, has the role of furthering and intensifying maturity of consciousness.

The capacity to receive GNA is determined by one's inner affinity with what is radiated by the code itself. GNA should correspond to the aspirations of those who receive it; thus individuals both attract it, and are attracted by it. The subtle action that this genetic code can carry out to fashion life according to the pulsation of the spirit is still a mystery to most people. It will continue to be a mystery until purity and surrender to the Higher Law, the Law of Love-Wisdom, has become the blueprint for human progress.

Once they have completed their earthly karma, the new human beings will have other resources available to them because their bodies will be purer, more sublime and divested of free will. With the new genetic code implanted in them, human beings will have greater access to Knowledge and will fulfill the tasks specified by the new law of evolution. They will express true love and will know that they are part of a harmony that integrates them, once and for all, into the order of the more advanced universes.

By aspiring to ascend to higher levels, without causing harm or transgressing the Law of Love, human beings will develop undisclosed potentialities. By obeying this sublime law, their own ascent will be assured and this will reflect on all humanity. They will live in unity more freely. Their lives will flow in the steadfast harmony of the spiritual levels of the cosmos that will finally be manifested here on Earth.

Awakening of the Right Side Consciousness

Excerpted from: Beyond Karma, by Trigueirinho

Human beings go through life building links to things, ideas, people, tendencies and forms of life. These links are registered in a part of human consciousness called the left side consciousness. The power of karma, as well as the inclination toward desire and other factors that have drawn this civilization into decadence, are also located in the left side consciousness.

Nevertheless, there is another part of human consciousness that is capable of bringing equilibrium to the tendencies of the left side consciousness and of establishing harmony with the higher laws. This is the right side consciousness, which creates linkages with the abstract levels where archetypal patterns and directives for the Plan of Evolution are revealed. The left side consciousness, in turn, pertains to acquiring knowledge through the external senses and to reproducing familiar patterns. Therefore, it infers association with concrete facts, trivial ideas and ordinary ways of living, perpetuated by customs and all kinds of traditions.

☙❧

Certain concepts regarding the etheric level of existence are important in order to understand the changes that will permit some humans to transcend the Law of Karma.

Electric circuits running through the etheric body convey the nerve impulses that reveal to the physical organs the kind of conduct needed to keep the whole organism functioning well. The etheric body also provides the force of cohesiveness for the physical body.

While agglomerations of cells form the organs of the physical body, which, in turn, comprise systems, the etheric body is made up of interconnected nuclei of energies. The level of one's physical health and harmony depends on the degree of clearness of these energy circuits.

There is a countless number of energy circuits in the etheric body, although not all are of equal importance. Some are pivotal while others rotate around them. The paths traced by energy in these circuits, as well as the nuclei activated in them, correspond to the human being's need for expression and for relationship with the surrounding universe.

These circuits are manifested according to each person's level of sensitivity and of spiritual maturity. In this way, the etheric body of someone who focuses on dense things is different from the etheric body of someone whose life is grounded in altruism. The energy centers in action in one body are different from those acting in another. But despite these individual aspects, there is one model for the etheric body of all the members of the human family during a given evolutionary cycle.

There are seven centers or vortices of energy located in the aura close to the spinal column in the etheric body of a human being who still has DNA genetic code and who is governed by the Law of Karma. These centers are called chakras.

Teachers of the past drew attention to these chakras and used them as a basis to present keys for conscious evolutionary work. For example, A Treatise on White Magic[1] points out that living a pure and upright life is the simplest form of adjusting the energies to evolutionary needs and of awakening dormant vital mechanisms and structures.

---

[1] Alice A. Bailey, A Treatise on White Magic [New York: Lucis Publishing Company, 1951].

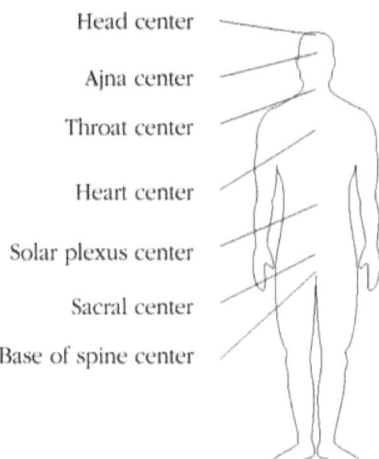

The seven chakras related to DNA genetic code

According to this teaching and to many others based on the system of chakras, the personality, which is the material aspect of the human being, reaches its peak when the latent energies at the base of the spine rise to the head and are carried to the center between the eyes, the ajna center. Later, when the energies from the sacral center are sublimated, reoriented and elevated to the throat center, and when the sexual drive has been transcended, the person becomes a conscious creator-force in the higher worlds. Furthermore, when the energies of the solar plexus become transmuted and reoriented to the heart center, the human being will attain group consciousness and become a server of humanity.

This was the work of energy elevation developed throughout the cycle presently coming to a close. However, nowadays this chakra circuit is being discontinued and a new circuit, that of the right side consciousness, is beginning to be activated in some pioneering individuals. The energy gradually shifts from one system to the other. To understand this process one must bear in mind that:

- Each stage of planetary development has a basic etheric structure, an archetypal pattern to be manifested;

- A new planetary and solar cycle began on 8/8/88 (August 8, 1988), with a period of intense purification on Earth and thus the levels of consciousness on the planet are undergoing profound transformations;
- A new genetic code will govern the formation of the bodies of today's human beings.

In this way, the energy potential available to humans is increasing, and the energy source which was formerly distributed through seven main centers (the chakras) is now concentrated in three centers — the right side mental center, the heart center and the cosmic plexus.

Later this potential will expand and two more centers, called supraluminaries, will be added to the three centers that have already become activated. If we look closely, we will see that this new energy system in humanity was already implicit in ancient teachings and, in an esoteric way, in the more advanced concepts of the sayings of spiritual sages, such as Sri Aurobindo. However, it was only with the transition that occurred on 8/8/88 (August 8, 1988), that these concepts were finally disclosed.

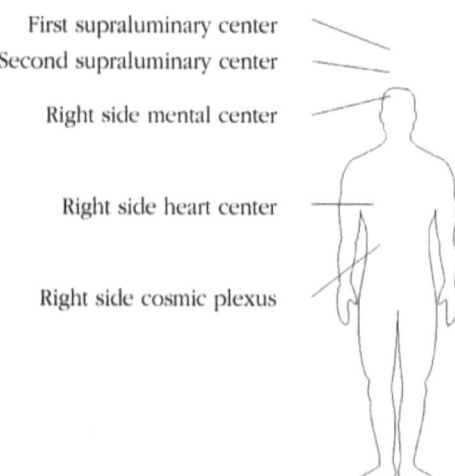

The centers of the right side consciousness related to the new genetic code

In the shift from the chakra system to the right side consciousness system, the energy from the head center, the ajna center and part of the throat center merges into a single center, the right side mental center. This is where the cognitive and creative capacities will be unified, bringing human beings greater equilibrium in their interaction with the outer world. Analytical and concrete mental activity will gradually move to the subconscious sphere and become automatic, similar to the organic functions of the physical body today.

Centers of the right side consciousness	Chakras that are being absorbed into the centers of the right side consciousness
Right side mental center	Head center Ajna center Throat center
Right side heart center	Throat center Heart center Solar plexus center
Right side cosmic plexus	Solar plexus center Sacral center Base of spine center

The energies channeled through the sacral and the base of the spine centers, as well as those channeled through the solar plexus, converge at the center located on the right side of the body, below the last rib, the cosmic plexus. Therefore, the sublimation of the instinctive aspects carried out by evolutionary work based on the system of chakras is being superseded. Individuals whose right side consciousness centers are activated will no longer have their energy focused on such a dense level and the raising of this energy will mean a much greater expansion of consciousness.

The right side heart center synthesizes the energy of the heart center of the former system of chakras and receives part of the energy of the solar plexus and of the throat center. The potential for impersonal love and for creativity will thus be united and will function together. This will totally change relationships among human beings. Difficulties stemming from self-centered interactions will no longer exist, for the heart center is more open to the vibration of the soul, the nucleus in which fraternal life is a reality.

The raising of the energy in these centers of a human being is a natural outcome of the shift in polarization of consciousness. Therefore, nothing should be done to induce it.[2] On the outer levels, the complete transfer from the former chakra system to the right side consciousness circuitry comes about through a spontaneous uplifting of energy, from the quelling of the ego and from the renunciation of free will. In this way, the forces of the ego become integrated into the energies of the soul, which makes it easier for individuals to acquire more self-control and to contact supraphysical laws, especially the higher law of evolution.

This brief account can give one an idea of the effect these transformations have upon transcending the Law of Karma. Everything that ties human beings to the chain of actions and reactions becomes permeated and governed by other, more subtle, laws. The quality of vibration, which the vortices of the right side consciousness bring about, enables a person to attune to frequencies that are above the ordinary ones of today.

Transition from the left side consciousness to the right side consciousness is not abrupt, for it accompanies an entire reorganization of the energy structure of the bodies of the personality (mental, emotional, and physical-etheric). Gradually a new way of looking at facts begins to emerge, replacing the former, more restricted and selfish way. One immediate outcome is that the awakening of the right side consciousness links a human being to laws that are more subtle than the Law of Karma, especially the higher law of evolution. The person enters a current into which the harmony in the universes can flow without impediment. Right side consciousness is based on communion and brings out the peaceful nature in beings, thus making it possible to vibrate on supraphysical and cosmic levels.

---

[2] See footnote on page 112.

Part Two

"Superior beings have come to this earth planet since ages ago; but, their work completed, they have gone away again. Since then, other visits have been made from different parts of outer space."

(Paul Brunton, The Notebooks of Paul Brunton: Reflections on my Life and Writing, vol. 8 [Burdett, NY: Larson Publications, 1987], page 224.)

"A new kingdom is coming into being; a fifth kingdom in nature is materialising, and already has a nucleus functioning on earth in physical bodies. Therefore let us welcome the striving and struggling of the present time, for it is a sign of resurrection."

(Alice A. Bailey, From Bethlehem to Calvary [New York: Lucis Trust, 1965], page 254.)

"It has been known for a long time by the mystics of all the world religions and by esoteric students everywhere, that certain members of the planetary Hierarchy are approaching closer to the earth at this time."

(Alice A. Bailey, The Externalization of the Hierarchy [New York: Lucis Trust, 1985], page 4.)

Planetary Centers

Excerpted from: Esoteric Lexicon, by Trigueirinho

Planetary centers are vortices that channel down to the Earth the energies and impulses emanated by the planetary Logos, the solar Logos or other broader cosmic sources. These centers are focal points of the universal energy of the planet since the supra-mental planes form the basis for their activity. They make it possible for light to permeate the various levels of terrestrial life and guide these levels toward the goals that are to be achieved.

Planetary centers act in unison, forming a subtle network through which the inner government of the planet is manifested. They are projected to intraterrestrial centers, intra-oceanic centers, spiritual centers and other active nuclei that are also on the surface of the Earth. The main planetary centers in these times are: Anu Tea, Aurora, Erks, Iberah, Lis-Fatima, Mirna Jad and Miz Tli Tlan.

The names of these planetary centers also designate intraterrestrial civilizations that are linked to them.

The energy circuit formed by those centers during this period can be represented by the octahedron, a geometric figure known since ancient times. The pyramids are based on this figure, which shows that in the past these constructions had a profound esoteric meaning, but they were only able to express part of the potentiality of the octahedron.

Currently the planetary centers have become interrelated according to the archetypal model of the octahedron. Thus the Earth has been given a way to draw closer to sacred patterns. The point of balance of these energy streams is to be found in Miz Tli Tlan, the regent center of the planet. These seven centers form triangular interactions that have an influence on the various levels of existence. The centers imprint the quality of the appropriate Ray[1] for each cycle on the matrix substance of the planet. By analogy, they are related to the planetary body in which they are found, in the same way that the etheric centers and certain organs are related to the human body.

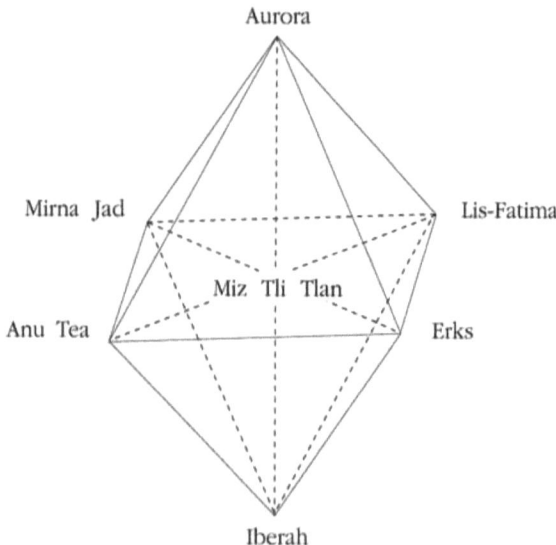

The octahedron represents the interrelationship among the planetary centers

Some of the relationships among planetary centers and Rays, with regard to their manifestation on terrestrial spheres are depicted in the following diagram and tables.

---

[1] Ray. One of the basic energies of the manifested universes. There are Seven Rays that work directly in the interweaving of life on the physical cosmic level of this solar system.

Planetary Centers

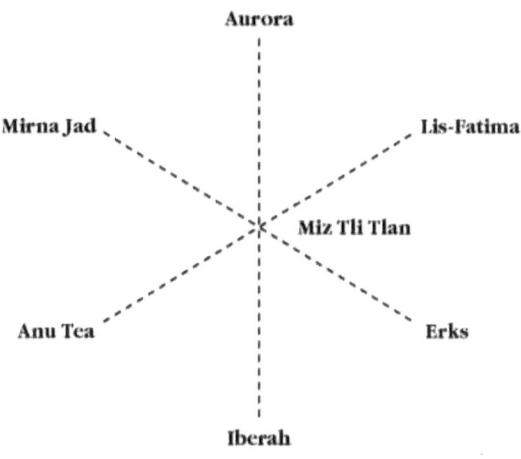

Axes of the octahedron

The interrelationship of the First, Second and Third Rays with the planetary centers corresponds to the axes of the octahedron:

Rays	Centers
First Ray (will-power)	Aurora/Miz Tli Tlan/Iberah
Second Ray (love-wisdom)	Mirna Jad/Miz Tli Tlan/Erks
Third Ray (active intelligence)	Lis-Fatima/Miz Tli Tlan/Anu Tea

Rays Four through Seven are expressed through the surfaces of the octahedron:

Rays	Centers that send the Ray energies to planetary life	Centers that receive the expression of the Ray energy from planetary life
Fourth	Iberah / Mirna Jad / Lis-Fatima	Aurora / Erks / Anu Tea
Fifth	Iberah / Erks / Anu Tea	Aurora / Lis-Fatima / Mirna Jad
Sixth	Aurora / Erks / Lis-Fatima	Iberah / Mirna Jad / Anu Tea
Seventh	Aurora / Mirna Jad / Anu Tea	Iberah / Lis-Fatima / Erks

Because the Earth is undergoing a process of cosmic evolution, other Rays, besides the seven mentioned above, will be revealed and manifested. New interrelationships will then be formed as a result of this.

The mirrors of these centers are linked to the Inner Schools and they remain in continual attunement with the nuclei of the solar system and with the constellations of the Zodiac.

Some correlations of the planetary centers on a cosmic scale:

Planetary center	Nuclei of the solar system	Constellations of the Zodiac
Anu Tea	Mercury and Saturn	Scorpio and Capricorn
Aurora	Saturn and Neptune	Sagittarius and Aries
Erks	Uranus and Saturn	Capricorn and Libra
Iberah	Mercury, Mars and Pluto	Cancer, Scorpio and Taurus
Lis	Moon, Venus and Jupiter	Gemini and Virgo
Mirna Jad	Venus and Neptune	Aquarius and Pisces
Miz Tli Tlan	Sun and Jupiter	Leo and Aquarius

Work on the supra-mental levels, where this attunement takes place, has an adaptability that has not yet been expressed in concrete life. Each action follows a perfect order, indefinable to the current human mind. Therefore, this information gives some indications but does not presume to cover the entire subject.

Spiritual Hierarchy

Excerpted from: Esoteric Lexicon,
by Trigueirinho

A Hierarchy is a group of consciousnesses that have transcended material evolution and have become integrated into service in the cosmic sense. A Hierarchy takes on the tasks of the Plan of Evolution and responds to the governing laws of the universes in which it works. It possesses the gift of omniscience and has attained union. It expresses a single Ray or a set of Rays and it may even manifest all the Rays to the extent required for service. The higher the level on which a Hierarchy is polarized, the wider are the spectrums of vibration it synthesizes and expresses.

Hierarchies exist throughout the cosmos and they form a network called the Brotherhood that transmits evolutionary impulses to various worlds. They are a part of the diverse kingdoms, such as the spiritual, the divine and the kingdom of the devas and the angels. These lives are consecrated by the Central Celestial Government and the law is fully applied through them.

A Hierarchy can more easily contact a human being who has awakened to standards of conduct that are in keeping with evolution. A Hierarchy takes into account everyone and everything, for each living spark is important to cosmic existence. It develops and instructs human consciousness, illuminating the way and stimulating deep nuclei, according to the capacity of each individual. It creates conditions for old ties to be severed, but in order to do so individuals themselves must give their permission and must not generate new ties that could aggravate the obscureness in which they are immersed.

Hierarchies differ from one another according to their level of evolution, to the vibrations and laws they express and to the tasks they carry out. They are energies, and at times they became manifested in order to reveal their existence and to work for the good of all. A Hierarchy is more than an individualized being; it represents a line of light that enfolds a myriad of consciousnesses on diverse levels. Furthermore, in each universe there is a nucleus formed by a decision of the Hierarchy's Logos,[1] which promotes the fulfillment of the goals of that universe. This nucleus is made up of various Hierarchies, but it is also referred to as Hierarchy—whether it be planetary, solar, galactic or cosmic.

It is up to humanity to recognize the energy of the Hierarchies with which it comes into contact. This recognition could then allow humanity to have a more profound relationship with the Hierarchies.

A Hierarchy can also be composed of a group of monads that have responded to the call to fulfill evolutionary tasks, acting as channels for the outpouring of the energies from planetary centers, planets or constellations.

It should be noted that the forces of involution are also organized hierarchically.

---

[1] Logos. A generic term for the central consciousness of a universe.

Cosmic, Intraterrestrial and Surface Races

*Excerpted from: Miz Tli Tlan —An Awakening World,
by Trigueirinho*

The following information comes from a member of the Alpha and Omega Council.

The cosmic and evolved extraterrestrial races have gained knowledge of all of the laws of the universe and they routinely follow these laws. This is why very advanced cosmic races are considered to be perfect by other races. The more evolved of the cosmic races are also able to control how the fulfillment of the law takes place within the Plan of Evolution. There are less developed extraterrestrial races as well.[1]

Inhabitants of the Earth should also serve the Law of Evolution, for this helps them attain higher levels and a greater evolution within the Law of Creation. However, still ignoring their planetary or cosmic origins, humans from the surface of the Earth go through life trying to decipher unimportant mental enigmas.

---

[1] See footnote: "Space Vessel" on page 8.

In the Law of Evolution one is not concerned with trying to achieve a perfect long life free of illness. The law deals with developing consciousness through the exercise of spiritual knowledge. It is spiritual knowledge that must be sought and not the preservation, at all costs, of the conditions of dense matter. The work with test tubes is part of the misguided thinking that will never produce a perfect human. It will only produce humans who respond to the laws of matter, and not to the nonmaterial laws.

The races of the surface are subject to the evolutionary cycles of life and death until they reach a consciousness of the more subtle planes of existence. However, the intraterrestrial races have life spans that exceed 650 years of your calendar. They have reached greater knowledge of how to coexist with the harmonious laws of nature. They use energies that do not produce aggressive impacts. This is different from what happens with your nuclear energy, which turns against its own users.

Terrestrial scientists made the mistake of using an energy without first having discovered the means to control it. In this way, they contaminated the planet. The planet would be in an even worse condition if it were not for the thousands of intergalactic vessels that work together continuously, carrying out a certain type of transmutation.

Another difference between the race of the surface and the intraterrestrial race is that the latter can travel to the various levels in this universe inhabited by intelligent and evolving beings. The intraterrestrial race has become integrated with Nature, respecting it and living together with it in a harmonious way unknown to you.

But if you are looking for a comparison between intraterrestrial and cosmic extraterrestrial races, you will find the distance between them even greater. Many from these races have been once and for all freed from the Law of Birth and Death. They have an incorporeal existence, which, however, can be made corporeal at will, the same as our representatives of Interplanetary and Intergalactic Councils, whose presence is no longer unknown to the inhabitants of the surface of the Earth. In spite of the efforts humanity has made to hide the fact of our presence, we continue to be here, working on a plan that we try to bring to you so that you also may fulfill it. We of the cosmic race are guided by a higher intelligence, whereas humanity of the surface, as you know, does not accept being guided. Humans are not aware that they are under evolutionary laws which are guided by higher races from the cosmos that have come here within the Law of Service to rescue humanity and to harmonize the Earth again.

Here are some widespread aggressions committed by humans of the surface:

1. They have released uncontrollable energy, which is exposing the life of humans and that of the planet to great cataclysms;
2. They have contaminated the waters of the planet, and there is very little potable water left for human consumption;
3. They have made the same mistake with pesticides, fungicides and herbicides as they did with nuclear energy, for they cannot control the level of the contamination produced in combating pests. Humans have no idea of the unknown illnesses caused by environmental contamination that they will have to face. If it were not for the intervention of our immense laboratory space vessels that are working to control the damages suffered by planet Earth due to the release of deadly forces, the civilization of the surface would be suffering still more than it does today.

But, as widespread as these erroneous human actions may be, there have always been the innocent ones whom the Law of Creation and the Law of Evolution of the races protect and save. It is also for their sake that we are here.

Space Vessels

Excerpted from: Oceans Can Hear,
by Trigueirinho

UFO is the acronym for Unidentified Flying Object, and in general it refers to space vessels, a reality that terrestrial science denies. It is used by those who are at a level of rational consciousness. Whereas, those who know about the existence of the inner world and are open to it, realize that there is no such thing as an unidentified flying object. Events and life are perceived in their essentialness, and mystery, as the mind calls it, is non-existent. Because these individuals are ready to recognize supraphysical realities, when they see a materialized intraterrestrial or extraplanetary vessel they know what it is about and need no explanations. They identify that sacred expression by the energy that emanates from it, by the inner communication that is beyond analytical or comparative mechanisms.

Some people attribute the appearance of these vessels to reflections of light in the atmosphere, others believe they are devices used in secret tests by the economically more powerful nations.

Because of misleading campaigns and widespread ignorance in this matter, the majority of the reporting and testimony on the attempts of humanities from other planets to approach humanity of the surface has been misrepresented and has even fallen into discredit.

As of 1988, however, the Hierarchies transmitted a new spiritual impulse in order to assist humanity in raising its consciousness and to prepare it for an effective relationship with space vessels, without any of the sensationalism associated with phenomena. Eventually this impulse was intensified. Now is the time for expansion and strengthening of the spiritual consciousness on the face of the Earth. The time has come for silent and mature work in which individuals go to profound levels of their cosmic essence, where they will find beings from other universes and other dimensions.

Individual evolutionary activity is being substituted by group efforts that are being permeated by this transforming impulse in an unusual manner. In recent times a special mobilization has been noted in the beings who, as a group, turn to spiritual life and dedicate themselves to selfless service. This mobilization should reflect the purpose of the world service network which, although it is on inner levels, acts principally through incarnated souls. However, most of these groups have remained crystallized in old tendencies, centered on their own process of development without effectively assuming their evolutionary tasks in the concrete world.

The basis on which supra-human energies can be anchored is the unification of beings dedicated to the Good, and not to traditional institutions or formal organizations. This unity is an impersonal entity, the qualities of which transcend the human sphere. This is the planetary or world service network referred to earlier.

Today many people are left without spiritual guidance even though they are seeking higher knowledge and trying to maintain balanced and harmonious lifestyles. They can receive significant help from intraterrestrial and extra-planetary vessels if they are receptive to it. This help, which is capable of harmonizing and healing them on the various levels where life unfolds, is always available and flows continually.

Water is the best element in the terrestrial material world to conduct magnetism. Since the materialization and dematerialization of the vessels, as well as their inter-dimensional transfer, are essentially magnetic processes, the proximity of great bodies of liquid helps them to use up less energy. This is why vessels are often seen near seas and lakes.

The intraterrestrial and intra-oceanic vessels are also capable of traveling through airspace. Some of them are linked to subtle bases that exist in the layers of the atmosphere. While each type has its features, in general these vessels are small, even when they can hold up to five smaller vessels inside them. On the other hand, extra-planetary vessels reach solar, galactic or extragalactic ranges and one of their characteristics is to move extremely quickly. For example, they enter the aura of the Earth in a materialized form and go toward the intraterrestrial centers at such a speed that they cannot even be seen and only leave luminous traces that are symbolic and inspirational lines in the sky.

The intraterrestrial, intra-oceanic or extra-planetary vessels are made up of the element of light. This element promptly responds to the commands of a higher intelligence and serves as intermediary for the essence of life to materialize in multiple gradations without becoming subject to the laws of the planes where it is manifested. This means that when the vessels cross the terrestrial atmosphere, be it psychic or physical, they do not generate material karma. They are therefore able to carry out their tasks freely.

Egotism is what mainly puts restraints on the contact of human beings with the vessels and subtle civilizations. In fact, it is not the elder brothers, members of more evolved human populations, who hide from terrestrial human beings, but rather it is the humans who isolate themselves from the subtle beings when they weave dense webbings of individualistic and material forces around themselves.[1]

---

[1] See A WORLD WITHIN A WORLD — X-7 Reporting — Transmissions from Russia on the Theory and Practice of Solar Light Radiations [Neville Spearman Ltd.: St. Helier, Jersey Island, 1981].

Our Role Today

Excerpted from: Oceans Can Hear,
by Trigueirinho

Individuals who really become aware of the current situation of the planet are inspired to evaluate their own life, values, goals and intentions. They begin to strive for higher standards of conduct, seeking an existence in harmony with all things.

While they often might want to struggle against chaos and the forces that generate it, they will realize that confrontation and fire by friction tend to create greater disharmony. They will begin to see the need to base their actions on higher laws and vibrations. They will then discover the power of solar fire and of cosmic fire that are present within them and in the entire universe. They will recognize the laws of supra-human evolution and will cooperate in the transfer of their own energy from the human to the spiritual plane.

During this process, which takes time as well as perseverance, the group consciousness that is characteristic of the soul begins to draw closer to the individual. Souls tend to seek others with whom they can fulfill stages of evolution and service. The energy that is generated in a group formed this way is greater than the sum total of the energy coming from each of its members. Therefore, an authentic group is more than just a gathering of individuals. In order for it to exist effectively, the group must have an impersonal common goal and must be entrusted with an evolutionary task. In this way the interaction of its members empowers the positive aspects of the whole group and becomes the channel through which impulses of great relevance for the transformation of planetary life can flow.

The entire surface of the Earth is in need of help to undergo transformation. Since the material levels, more than any other, are the most resistant to change, it has been observed that help is only effective and causes less conflict when it comes from the Most High. Sometimes people with good intentions who have not yet reached certain levels of maturity in their inner life try in vain to promote movements with altruistic aims. A firm and consolidated spiritual base is needed to form a clear link with the Hierarchy and to avoid transitory and ephemeral movements, so that the Work may be fulfilled.

Choices for Evolution

Excerpted from: Oceans Can Hear,
by Trigueirinho

There are decisions which, if made within the silence of the self, give impetus to one's ascesis and attune one to spiritual laws. These become possible when the goals of inner life are recognized by the conscious self, inspiring it to follow the direction indicated by its deep inner core. The decisions need not be announced to the world; they are part of a dynamic process and are confirmed as one continues to walk the path. They are true inner vows directly linked to the initiations, for they contribute to a clarification of the goal to be achieved. Any openness to what is evolutionary in the universe helps to strengthen these decisions.

According to spiritual law, with each regressive attitude one comes to a halt in one's advancement along the cosmic path. At every instant there is a choice to be made between what is evolutionary and what is involutionary. As long as an individual gives way to free will and remains within the sphere of human and material laws, he or she will have to depend on personal discernment. But once free will is transcended, that is, when the monadic will begins to take precedence over personal ideas and desires, the individual can have an intuitive insight or receive a sign as to what direction should be taken. Furthermore, a greater wisdom adjusts the events of one's external life so that it may have a greater energy level. The development of serene vigilance is of great help in situations where human discernment alone must be used as a test for the conscious self, as well as in those cases where signs clearly come from inner levels.

One must remember that the choices to be made vary from individual to individual. They depend on what must be transcended, developed or deepened. We cannot say in general terms what must be done in order to cooperate in planetary transformations. But we can be aware that the transmuting energies, which permeate the Earth at this time can penetrate our being. If we allow them to, these energies can raise our vibrations at any moment.

At this time in which the terrestrial world is going through upheavals and is preparing for intense purification, it is necessary to be firmly united to the life of the spirit—omniscience, omnipresence and freedom. To attain this unity, this pure love, one must ardently surrender and wholeheartedly dedicate oneself to the One Consciousness, origin and destiny of all things.

Part Three

"For a high-spiritual development, not only the opening of the centers is essential but their transmutation also…"

(Helena Roerich, Letters of Helena Roerich, vol. I [New York: Agni Yoga Society, 1939], page 426.)

"We rejoice when the step of true cooperation is reached; then the smallest sign is understood."

(Agni Yoga Society, Supermundane—The Inner Life, Book One, # 60 [New York: Agni Yoga Society, 1938], page 104.)

"The fiery energies are reaching Earth toward the appointed time, and we may expect great changes, which must bring the awakening of the spirit. […] The new race is being born."

(Helena Roerich, Letters of Helena Roerich, vol. II [New York: Agni Yoga Society, 1940], page 75.)

An Exercise to Develop the Right Side Consciousness

From: Miz Tli Tlan —An Awakening World,
by Trigueirinho

In order to interpret universality with total freedom, one must transcend the material levels of existence. It is impossible to reach deep understanding if we remain bound by the three-dimensional consciousness, limited to the physical, emotional and mental planes. Unless we become freed from earthly ties, from the left side consciousness and from everyday life, our consciousness cannot contact the intelligent worlds that inhabit the infinite universe.

If we limit ourselves to the corporeal dimension of beings on the material level, we will be nurturing an ephemeral creature that is subject to birth and death, to pain, to desire and to suffering, which are all present, as much in the decadence as in the advancement of the races. These situations are inherent to three-dimensional consciousness. All those who are now ready are being offered the means to transcend the current conditions and to move toward the divine essence.

The next stage that humans are to attain is on a cosmic level. To reach this stage one must cease giving in to the ignorant mind and must transcend it until reaching the supra-mind. The substance of the supra-mind is a component of the spiritual formation of the self. A still higher cosmic level will then move humans to seek the spirit and to transcend their soul, which will no longer be identified with human life in itself but will be absorbed into this spirit. This is the vibration of Miz Tli Tlan.

If beings do not overcome their body and control their physical composition and all their material existence, they cannot perceive universal consciousness. There is no fully conscious oneness unless the left side mind is completed by the right side mind. The left side consciousness embodies the present limits of human thought, which is not integrated into the universal mind. The awakening of the right side consciousness and its merging with the left side consciousness will allow humans to avail themselves of unity with all other minds and with the universal mind. This will take place gradually.

This new state leads to universality, but to attain it one must go beyond everything that is earthly. This cannot be reiterated often enough. Mind, life and humankind have all been created to reach supra-nature, which will become part of human thought, feeling and action. All of this will indeed take place. The three greater mirrors of Miz Tli Tlan, Aurora and Erks, within the broader sphere of the Hierarchies and of Amuna Khur, will bring about the awakening.

This awakening is impossible without an inner life. The activation of the three centers, the right side mental center, the right side heart center and the right side cosmic plexus, will help express cosmic consciousness. When these centers become activated, individuals will find the way to truly identify themselves with greater existence. Life that is lived apart from the inner spirit is simply the domain of ignorance. This ignorance can only be dispelled through awareness of inner cosmic life.

Detachment from the self will become integrated into the culture of the race. New knowledge in the fields of astronomy, physics and religiousness is to be revealed. Religiousness in this context does not mean any affiliation with church institutions, but rather obedience to the set of laws that gives human beings knowledge of the essence of all the inhabitants of this planet and of their stages of evolution and involution. Among other things, religiousness unveils the laws that govern the reorganization of the Hierarchies that are active on the planet.

The mind linked to the left side consciousness has always strived to attain balance in personal life by attachment to external reality, believing that material existence was the only basic reality. Only with great effort can one unravel the confused plot of external reality. However, with tranquil endeavor, one can reach the light of the mirrors.

By outer consciousness is meant human material consciousness, united with the individuality of one's being through the triple attunement with the mental, emotional and physical-etheric bodies. People can only become freed from this outer consciousness through a change of the present genes[1] and by breaking down the current structures that bind them. Solar forces of great potency are approaching to destroy the structures that shackle humans. Thus they will open the way for individuals to attain divine life inwardly.

Detachment from self is a movement toward one's inner being, so that the intraterrestrial call may come forth. If human beings of the surface change their interests, turning their attention away from the outer material plane and focusing it on the inner spiritual plane, not only will their thought structures be transformed but they will also discover the way to the universal mind. The awakening of the mind of right side consciousness will lead them to the correct inward movement. No longer will they be concerned with their own obscurity, nor will they avidly seek experiences. A broader vision will direct their abilities inward and everything in them will become harmonized.

Silence and emptiness will lead the beings to the infinite. This will be part of their inner spiritual experience that will reach the space where the physical mind refuses to enter. This tiny left side thinking mind confuses silence with mental and vital incapacity and considers void to mean the termination of existence. True silence is the silence of the nonmaterial plane. True void is the divestment of the natural being, a liberation from old conceptualizations in order to reach divine essence.

The greatest triumph that we will have achieved as the race of the surface of the Earth will be to attain knowledge of the intraterrestrial and the extraterrestrial races, knowledge of a different reality. Through our outer consciousness we are subjected to the separation that exists on the surface of the Earth between us and the others, main-

---

[1] This process is carried out on supraphysical levels by cosmic consciousnesses that watch over the evolution of humanity in the diverse manifested Universes.

ly members of the cosmic races who contact us. However, humans still cling to this separateness in order to satisfy the ego.

Individuals and groups who inhabit the surface of the Earth may carry out the activity of the mirrors in order to establish a conscious relationship with the other races. The following exercise with colors is an appropriate method to prepare for this today. Some exercises with colors have been especially created for beings in service who are in feminine physical bodies and are dedicated to work with the mirrors. However, the exercise with colors presented here has been formulated for individuals or groups in general.[2]

This exercise is called SHAMUNA, a word in the Irdin language and one of the names for God. In this age it refers to development toward transcendence of the three-dimensional being so as to be able to approach the races beyond the world of the surface.

೧೮೦

The exercise with colors corresponds to the harmony, integration and development of the new cosmic being. When it is practiced as a group, it should be guided by a competent coordinator in an orderly way. The work is carried out in silence and inner tranquility, in the morning or at night, without any expectations as to results.

First of all, attune to the Alpha and Omega Council and request permission to carry out this task. Next, invoke the presence of the greater Hierarchies of the planetary centers who correspond to the colors violet (Aurora), orange (Erks) and yellow (Miz Tli Tlan) used in the exercise.[3]

---

[2] This exercise does not induce the artificial awakening of the centers, but prepares the individual's magnetic field to receive new energies in attunement with the higher transformations that are taking place on the planet.

[3] The colors used here to attune with the potential of each center are not fixed, for they depend on the level of consciousness to be activated and on the task to be carried out.

An Exercise to Develop the Right Side Consciousness

Then mentally visualize the first color, violet. Breathe in, guiding the energy of the color and directing it from the right side mental center to the heart center on the right side of the body. Breath out when reaching the heart center. Breathe in again, visualizing the second color, orange, and send it from the heart center to the right side cosmic plexus. Breathe out when reaching the cosmic plexus. Breathe in once more, visualizing the third color, yellow, and send the energy of that color to the heart center. Breath out when reaching the heart center. Breathe in for the fourth time, visualizing the color of the heart center, orange, and send its energy to the right side mental center.

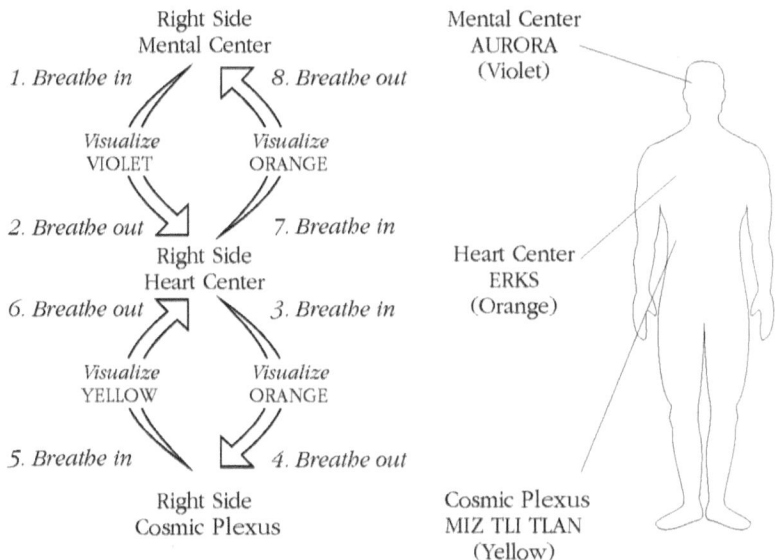

Sequence of the exercise with colors

The complete exercise, which begins and ends in the right side mental center, is done 10 times, using violet, orange, yellow and orange, and following the sequence of the right side mental center, heart center, cosmic plexus, heart center and right mental center. When the exercise is completed, remain in surrender to the light. Those who practice the above exercise will gain a better understanding of their own task in this planetary cycle.

Once having completed the exercise with the colors, initiates will be working with the three-dimensional forces of their bodies and will have integrated them into the three mirrors, since each color corresponds to a mirror. As for students, after the exercise has been carried out they will have attained much greater self-control.

The following words have been given by an intraterrestrial being from Miz Tli Tlan and may be used to help deepen this practice:

You live in a time of awakening.

Your quest is not yours alone, but it is to be sought together with others.

It is a quest for the true state of your being.

Do not return to the past, for if you do, you will set limits on your memory. Do not limit yourself to bodily form or to appearances.

Your being is in continual contact with other beings.

The limitations in which you are immersed today are not within the Law of the Spirit, but are temporary conditions of material manifestation.

You must create an opening to supra-consciousness, to the inner and higher being. You must rise above this identity with the physical body and eliminate concern as to what level you have already attained.

When the physical body has been dissolved or abandoned, there is one life after another, one world after another.

When you transcend your physical body you become a traveler of the new mind. In this state, unknown circumstances and results begin to be manifested for you. When projected outside of the physical body, be careful not to fall into idolatry. Cast yourself into your inner being where the Light shines outward.

When you do so, each individual and all the group will understand that higher values are not the same values as those of the three-dimensional world.

Change your state of consciousness, change it now.

Through this exercise with the colors you can achieve this goal. This exercise is to be done by those who feel inclined to do it.

I send Love and Light to you and to your groups.

Tasks for the New Human

Excerpted from: Erks—Inner World, by Trigueirinho

Individual Tasks

When I speak to you of individual tasks, I am referring to your attunement with the right side consciousness.

You are on the threshold of great change. Individual tasks exist in order for you to attain mastery of the attunement with the regent, or monad. After that, you will really be able to serve through group service.

To serve, you must remain in the haven of Divine Love within your soul and, in silence, send out thoughts of invisible help and enthusiasm.

Here are some basic affirmations for this work:

I will endeavor to change to a more subtle dimension and then, formless and nameless, be the contacted messenger, who, in divine peace, journeys through the obscure facets of thought, setting alight the flame of peace wrought in the forges of cosmic silence.

Once I have reached other planes, I will help the infirm to gain health and peace.

I will also guide my fellow beings and help them to be strong, so that they can find suitable work and be useful.

I will seek the etheric substance to build the temple of my soul and I will be aware that God dwells therein.

I will share with others the fruit of my cosmic devotion so that they may stay attuned and may feel immensely peaceful.

I will serve in spirituality and with joy.

Group Tasks

Through cosmic grace you will be freed from your heavy burdens of flesh and bones and will sever that which shackles the body; you will break free will. All this will be done with the help of the monad that dwells in cosmic space.

Basic Affirmations

We are already free, and basing ourselves on inner life, we will seek the tasks that are required of us through group service.

We will live the beauty of the path, without straying from the goal either with our eyes or with our thoughts.

The melodies of the Universe will integrate us into their tones and together we will share the fruits that we must prepare.

We will inhale the fragrance of the geraniums, the lilies, the carnations, the roses and the jasmines; we will not be distracted when the Hierarchies guide us toward the Divine Dwelling Place in the Cosmos, where the Space Gardeners await.

We will overcome the allure of the senses, which used to engage us in deceptive thoughts and were obstacles to subtle perceptions.

Our bonds with the flesh have been broken. This has allowed us to become travelers of the Kingdom, where we are being awaited to carry out the tasks for the coming times.

When we have built an altar in our hearts, we will contemplate the work to be offered up.

We will return the fruits of our work to the energy centers of our being and to the stream of life which, through the heart, will permeate the entire liberated body.

Then, soundlessly, our being will journey along a sacred internal river, following the spiral to the Kingdom of the Spirit, dwelling place of the monad.

A New Dawn

Excerpted from: The Voice of Amhaj,
by Trigueirinho

Human consciousness does not need to be limited to the environs of this solar system. It should expand, reach distant universes and merge into their energies. Such a journey is not taken in rockets, but in spirit. Our space vessels are live manifestations of consciousness; they are light. Therefore, for them, time and space have no limits. If human beings knew the immensity that awaits them perhaps they would be more willing to seek the law. The law abides in one's inner self. So, first of all, frontiers are transcended within and later this is reflected in material life. Terrestrial life cries out for freedom and in response to this plea, We are present and active. Build your fortress with the unassailable energy of the spirit. For this, you have My Ray. And this is why you know My Name.

☙❧

Each planet corresponds to a stage of universal evolution. No two planets are alike and the same occurs with individuals. Cosmic creativity is infinite and reveals its power in manifold forms. The transubstantiation of terrestrial matter is already underway, but it needs vastness to be developed. This vastness is the fruit of purity and thus all the corners of the Earth will be washed. My Ray participates actively in this process, opening the pathway to eternity. The future is as near to you as breathing. The chronology of events is no more than a conditioning that is surpassed as soon as consciousness penetrates the spiritual kingdom. Hence, We invite you to give wings to your heart and soar toward the Infinite.

☙❧

The density that currently prevails in the terrestrial sphere hinders one's perception of the rays of the planets and stars. However, these rays are always present and active, like the Sun on a cloudy day. The disciple should rise above the clouds and contact these rays, recognizing their different vibrations. Learn how to attune to them and transmit them to the material plane. This training takes place under Our supervision; self-surrender and detachment are also necessary. A chalice must be emptied in order to be filled; a bell must be free of sediment to vibrate fully when sounded. Glorious times are coming, but the planet must be prepared for them.

☙❧

Some humans have already crossed the frontiers of the Sun, even though humanity as a whole has remained prisoner of the planet. Here you have a key: the terrestrial circle was insurmountable for those human beings who were prisoners of the Earth, but not for those who knew how to fly. These teachings have always been transmitted to the few elect who, in silence, followed the path of the Initiations. In these times the Earth opens its doors to neighboring universes because the freedom of the future has been assured by the Councils. This is why these times are precious and We can more widely unveil realities which were hidden before. Those who hear, understand.

☙❧

Much of what We transmitted to you in the past is no longer valid today. The Teaching was not wrong, but human consciousness has expanded and can now encompass a broader view. Those who have penetrated the aura of Truth know that Its essence is untouchable. The closer one comes to this essence, the deeper It gets. Thus, flexibility and detachment are once more recommended. To follow the ascent of the spirit requires vigor.

☙❧

Truth is relative to the boundaries within which one's consciousness abides. This is why the awakened pilgrim always renews his or her standards accordingly. No matter how beautiful the weaving might be, the genuine artisan is never satisfied.

◊

Fiery progression exponentially fuels the power of those who answer the Call positively. Their flaming armor is fortified under the arrows of the enemy. Their determination heralds the new Earth. But there are those who did not want to recognize the urgency of these times. They preferred the lethargy of a sick civilization in which even the best standards are interwoven with darkness. I call you to ardent conquest. I call you to service. I enounce your Name. Come, O Children of the Sun!

◊

The inappropriate intermingling of vibrations, so common on your planet in these days, must be promptly replaced by a magnetic selectivity. The capacity to wield it is developed through aspiration, surrender and, above all, discernment. Discernment is born from the fusion of the energies in the centers of the head and the heart; hence, silence is necessary. Recognize the importance of rhythm and conduct correctly the strands of light that the Hierarchy sends to you.

◊

The power of selfless action is immeasurable. Its radiation crosses frontiers and reaches the most distant universes. Now that the final moments of this cycle are drawing near on the material plane, horror will take over the stage of human life. Pure faith and selflessness are needed. The spirit is immortal, but one must allow it to ascend.

◊

Up to now the mantle of life has been woven with threads of grief and suffering on the surface of the Earth. Through their choices people could learn to distinguish the bad from the good and the good from the right. But now it is necessary to change the woven pattern, and for this reason you are living moments of intense trials. No longer grief and suffering, but a firm determination to advance will trace the pattern of this weaving.

༺༻

There have always been those who devoted their lives entirely to the Supreme Lord of the universes. They opened pathways for humanity; they were pillars of strength to sustain the planet. This total dedication is the sign of those who know and are unified with the Law of the Hierarchy. Our rays are not granted to the lukewarm or to the hypocrites, but to those who truly love the light.

༺༻

Surrender of the ego is vital for the liberation of the spirit. The spirit cannot fly freely as long as it maintains a disintegrating ego vortex on Earth. The higher will must absorb that which is below it. This is the law. In these times this law transports humanity to new kingdoms beyond the dark swamp of free will.

༺༻

You have recognized correctly the approach of Our Messenger. But greater detachment is needed. It is necessary to relinquish ideas and expectations. All that you know must be left aside. You must be empty, not wanting anything. We know you deeply; there is nothing that you can hide from Us. So, keep your inner flame burning, since the Messenger will soon return.

༺༻

Great is the responsibility of those who walk the path, but even greater are the blessings they receive. The light of tomorrow reflects in the mirror of their hearts and thus spreads to the whole planet. Yes, each link of this chain of light is important to fulfill the task. Success depends not only on the power of the Source, which is boundless, but also on the determination and readiness of those who receive it. In these times, when dense fog hides the rays of the Sun, one must know how to discern. May the disciples not be discouraged when facing difficulties; but may they use their difficulties to whet the edge of their sword.

༄༅

Whoever gets discouraged when attacked by the enemy is not ready to stand under the pure brilliance of light. As metal turns red when immersed in fire, the aura of those who seek the truth should be incandescent. To journey in this planet the spirit must be a warrior and its decision to go forward must be firm. Its armor is forged in devotion to the Supreme Lord and the sign of the chosen shines on its forehead. Warrior of the Light, Our Peace is your sustainment!

༄༅

Many students, when facing a new phase of the Teachings, look for proofs in the previous one. There is only one essence. But only the seeds of the incoming phase can be found in the previous one. Students must turn within. There they will find all the proofs needed.

༄༅

The evolutionary governance of the planet comes from the inner planes. Its true Hierarchy is composed of different levels of light. Humanity is being called to transcend the veils that hide these sublime realities and to cooperate in the manifestation of new times. This is why the existence of seven major centers was revealed to you and why Our Messengers so often draw near to you. The opportunity of these times is unique. Blessed be those who, though immersed in terrestrial darkness, believe in the light of dawn.

⊗

The Work is unending, its roots go deep into eternity. Each step taken becomes the base for the next one and ongoing ascent enlivens those who participate in it. Therefore, warn those who arrive—they must let themselves be permeated by the ardent fire of supreme devotion; they must die to themselves; they must serve only one Lord. The sublime glory blesses those who thus surrender to the power of the spirit. In their flight they will reach the most distant Dwellings.

⊗

I do not lift all of the veils since the time has not yet come. You should follow the path step by step; in it you will find guidance and protection. I know every inch of this narrow path and I assure that I am with you. When darkness becomes even denser, remember: the light is near. Reaffirm your vows and go ahead. Do not give in to the allurements of the past; many depend upon your victory.

⊗

Heralds of a new dawn, you are the messengers of Light! Under your bare feet flows the stream of power and love which will renew the face of the planet. With your hands We are building the temple that will shelter the liberated spirit. In your hearts the robes of the new humanity are being woven with threads of eternity. We strengthen the flow of the current of Good. We affirm the Supreme Will. Yes, We bless those who answer the Call.

The Pocket Book Series

The Light Within You
Doorway to a Kingdom
We Are Not Alone
Winds of Spirit
Finding the Temple
There Is Peace
Path Without Shadows

TRIGUEIRINHO

This is an English translation of a series of seven pocket books that were assembled with the aim of summarizing some of the information contained in the books published since 1987. Inspired by these books, spiritual study groups have begun gathering in various countries for prayer and reflection and the development of their inner potential.

Each book in this series has a way of sparking the impulse to enter the essence of one's being, to become one with the inner world. Although each book is complete in itself and independent of the others, together they represent a journey directing the reader to a new stage in his or her life. This collection is intended for those who feel called to imbue their lives with the sublime principles of purification.

BEYOND KARMA

TRIGUEIRINHO

As human beings grow in consciousness, their understanding of the Law of Karma also grows. They no longer see it as a mere instrument to compensate for past errors, but recognize it as an infallible means to fulfill the higher goal of life. They begin to notice that the Law of Karma is present on various levels of existence and that it functions in different ways.

Thus, they begin to cooperate with it intelligently. They are no longer performers of their destiny, but effective assistants of evolution, true co-creators.

About Trigueirinho and His Work

Jose Trigueirinho Netto (1931-2018) was born in Sao Paulo, Brazil. He lived in Europe for a number of years, where he maintained contact with individuals who were advanced on the spiritual path, including Paul Brunton.

In his own life he was an example of the teachings that he transmitted through his books and talks about the transcendence and elevation of the human being, the contact with the soul and with even more profound nuclei of the being, impersonal service, and the link with the Spiritual Hierarchies.

One of the fundamental elements of his work is to stimulate the expansion of human consciousness and to liberate it from the bonds that keep it imprisoned to material aspects of existence, both external and internal.

He was the Founder of the Community of Light Figueira (http://www.comunidadefigueira.org.br) and a Founder and member of the Board of Directors of the Fraternity International

Humanitarian Federation (www.fraterinternacional) as well as a Co-Founder of the Grace Mercy Order, an ecumenical Christian monastic order. He also was an active collaborator, instructor and spiritual protector of three other communities located in Uruguay, Argentina and Portugal.

In his last 30 years he lived in the Community of Light Figueira, in the interior of Minas Gerais, Brazil, a community that at present has approximately 300 residents and which is visited annually by thousands of collaborators who are members of a larger network of humanitarian services and of spiritual studies that was always guided and followed closely by Trigueirinho.

Thanks to his inestimable instruction and his love for the Kingdoms of Nature and as a result of the exemplary work that he himself implanted in the Figueira community, the Animal, Vegetable and Mineral Kingdoms are the recipients of loving treatment there.

Trigueirinho wrote over 80 books, published originally in Portuguese, with many of them translated into Spanish, English, French and German. He gave more than 3,000 talks that were recorded live and which are available in CD, with some available in DVD and pen drive. Approximately 100 of these recorded talks are available with English voice over at the website of the Shasti Association: http://www.shasti.org/instruction (drop down the menu tab titled "Trigueirinho Instruction" and then click on "MP3 audios").

The primary focus of the first phase of Trigueirinho's work was concerned with self-knowledge, prayer, instruction and spiritual transformation. Following this, he began to transmit information with respect to Universal Life and about the assistance that humanity has from its beginnings received by means of the Intra-terrestrial White Brotherhood which inhabits the Retreats and the Planetary Centers as well as through the Cosmic Brotherhood of the Universe. He provides information about the presence of the Spiritual Hierarchy on the planet and the advent of the new humanity.

His work also includes themes relating to: the need for humanity to balance the negative karmas that it has created in relation to the Kingdoms of Nature; the negative karmic burden that we carry from the history of slavery and the genocide of indigenous peoples; and the nature of spiritual work in groups. He also addresses issues of healing, a larger vision of astrology, the esoteric nature of symbols, sound and colors, and the divine feminine.

In his last eight years he analyzed with clarity and with the wisdom that always characterized him, the messages that the Divinity has been giving to the planet as a warning to humanity (available from www.mensajerosdivinos.org/en).

His work reveals a real comprehension of the significance of all the Kingdoms of Nature on our planet, the true spiritual task of the human being, its place in the universe and also its responsibility before Creation.

Finally, he clarifies the reasons for the crisis that today is devastating humanity, teaching how to avoid reacting negatively to an immanent natural catastrophe by contacting more subtle levels of consciousness, and opening perspectives for the beginning of a more luminous cycle for our race.

Books by Trigueirinho

(Books available in English have English title first)

Published by Editora Pensamento
Sao Paulo, Brazil

1987

Nossa Vida Nos Sonhos
OUR LIFE IN DREAMS

A Energia Dos Raios Em Nossa Vida
THE ENERGY OF THE RAYS IN OUR LIVES

1988

Do Irreal Ao Real
FROM THE UNREAL TO THE REAL

Hora de Crescer Interiormente
O Mito de Hércules Hoje
TIME FOR INNER GROWTH – *The Myth of Hercules Today*

A Morte Sem Medo e Sem Culpa
DEATH WITHOUT FEAR AND WITHOUT GUILT

Caminhos Para a Cura Interior
PATHS TO INNER HEALING

1989

ERKS – *Mundo Interno*
ERKS – *The Inner World*

Miz Tli Tlan – *Um Mundo que Desperta*
MIZ TLI TLAN – *A World that Awakens*

Aurora – Essência Cósmica Curadora
AURORA – *Cosmic Essence of Healing*

Signs of Contact
SINAIS DE CONTATO

O Novo Começo do Mundo
THE NEW BEGINNING OF THE WORLD

A Quinta Raça
THE FIFTH RACE

Padrões de conduta para a nova Humanidade
PATTERNS OF CONDUCT FOR THE NEW HUMANITY

Novos Sinais de Contato
NEW SIGNS OF CONTACT

Os Jardineiros do Espaço
THE SPACE GARDENERS

1990

A Busca da Síntese
THE SEARCH FOR SYNTHESIS

Noah's Vessel
A NAVE DE NOÉ

Tempo de Retiro e Tempo de Vigília
A TIME OF RETREAT AND A TIME OF VIGIL

1991

Portas do Cosmos
GATEWAYS OF THE COSMOS

Encontro Interno – *A Consciência-Nave*
INNER ENCOUNTER – *The Consciousness Space Vessel*

A Hora do Resgate
THE TIME OF RESCUE

O Livro Dos Sinais
THE BOOK OF SIGNS

Mirna Jad – *Santuário Interior*
MIRNA JAD – *Inner Sanctuary*

As Chaves de Ouro
THE GOLDEN KEYS

1992

Das Lutas à Paz
FROM STRUGGLE TO PEACE

A Morada Dos Elisíos THE ELYSIAN DWELLING PLACE

Hora de Curar – *A Existência Oculta*
TIME FOR HEALING – *The Occult Existence*

O Ressurgimento de Fátima Lis
THE RESURGENCE OF FATIMA LIS

História Escrita nos Espelhos
Princípios de Comunicação Cósmic
HISTORY WRITTEN IN THE MIRRORS -
Principles of Cosmic Communication

Passos Atuais
STEPS FOR NOW

Viagem por Mundos Sutis
TRAVEL THROUGH SUBTLE WORLDS

Segredos Desvelados – *Iberah e Anu Tea*
UNVEILED SECRETS – *Iberah and Anu Tea*

A Criação – *Nos Caminhos da Energia*
CREATION – *On the Paths of Energy*

The Mystery of the Cross In the Present Planetary Transition
O MISTÉRIO DA CRUZ NA ATUAL TRANSIÇÃO PLANETÁRIA

O Nascimento da Humanidade Futura
THE BIRTH OF THE FUTURE HUMANITY

1993

Aos Que Despertam
TO THOSE WHO AWAKEN

Paz Interna em Tempos Críticos
INNER PEACE IN CRITICAL TIMES

A Formação de Curadores
THE FORMATION OF HEALERS

Profecias aos Que Não Temem Dizer Sim
PROPHECIES FOR THOSE WHO ARE NOT AFRAID TO SAY YES

THE VOICE OF AMHAJ
A VOZ DE AMHAJ

O VISITANTE – O CAMINHO PARA ANU TEA
THE VISITOR –*The Way to Anu Tea*

A CURA DA HUMANIDADE
THE HEALING OF HUMANITY

OS NÚMEROS E A VIDAS – *Uma Nova Compreensão da Simbologia Oculta nos Números*
NUMBERS AND LIFE – *A New Understanding of Occult Symbolism in Numbers*

NISKALKAT – *Uma Mensagem para os Tempos de Emergência*
NISKALKAT – *A Message for Times of Emergency*

ENCONTROS COM A PAZ
ENCOUNTERS WITH PEACE

NOVOS ORÁCULOS
NEW ORACLES

UM NOVO IMPULSO ASTROLÓGICO
A NEW ASTROLOGICAL IMPULSE

1994

BASES DO MUNDO ARDENTE – *Indicações para Contato com os Mundos suprafíscicos*
BASES OF THE FIERY WORLD – *Indications for Contacts with Supraphysical Worlds*

CONTATOS COM UM MONASTÉRIO INTERATERRENO
CONTACTS WITH AN INTRATERRESTRIAL MONASTERY

Os oceanos têm Ouvidos
OCEANS HAVE EARS

A Trajetória do Fogo
THE PATH OF FIRE

Glossário Esotérico
ESOTERIC LEXICON

1995

The Light Within You
A LUZ DENTRO DE TI

1996

Doorway to a Kingdom
PORTAL PARA UM REINO

Beyond Karma
ALÉM DO CARMA

1997

We Are Not Alone
NÃO ESTAMOS SÓS

Winds of the spirit
VENTOS DO ESPÍRITO

Finding the Temple
O ENCONTRO DO TEMPLO

There is Peace
A PAZ EXISTE

1998

Path Without Shadows

CAMINHO SEM SOMBRAS

Mensagens para Uma Vida de Harmonia

MESSAGES FOR A LIFE OF HARMONY

1999

Toque Divino

THE DIVINE TOUCH

Coleção Pedaços de Céu

BITS FROM HEAVEN COLLECTION

- **Aromas do Espaço**
  AROMAS FROM SPACE
- **Nova Vida Bate à Porta**
  A NEW LIFE AWAITS YOU
- **Mais Luz No Horizonte**
  MORE LIGHT ON THE HORIZON
- **O Campanário Cósmico**
  THE COSMIC CAMPANILE
- **Nada Nos Falta**
  WE LACK NOTHING
- **Sagrados Mistérios**
  SACRED MYSTERIES
- **Ilhas de Salvação**
  ISLANDS OF SALVATION

2002

Calling Humanity

UM CHAMADO ESPECIAL

2004

És Viajante Cósmico
YOU ARE A COSMIC WAYFARER

Impulsos
IMPULSES

2005

Pensamentos para Todo o Ano
THOUGHTS FOR THE WHOLE YEAR

2006

Trabalho Espiritual com a Mente
SPIRITUAL WORK WITH THE MIND

Published by Editora Irdin
Carmo da Cachoeira, Minas Gerais, Brazil

2009

Signs of Blavatsky – *An Unusual Encounter for the Present Time*
SINAIS DE BLAVATSKY – *Um Inusitado Encontro nos Dias de Hoje*

2012

Consciências e Hierarquias
CONSCIOUSNESSES AND HIERARCHIES

2015

Mensagens Reunidas
COLLECTED MESSAGES

Mensagens para Sua Tranformaçã
MESSAGES FOR YOUR TRANSFORMATION

2017

Páginas de Amor e Compreensão
PAGES OF LOVE AND COMPREHENSION

2018

Novos Tempos: Nova Postura
NEW TIMES: NEW ATTITUDE

2020

Versos Livres
OBRA PÓSTUMA

Trigueirinho's works are published by:

Associação Irdin Editora – www.irdin.org.br (selected titles of books in English, Spanish and Portuguese and CDs in several languages), Carmo da Cachoeira, MG, Brazil.

Editora Pensamento – www.pensamento-cultrix.com.br (titles in Portuguese), São Paulo, SP, Brazil

Editorial Kier – www.kier.com.ar (selected titles in Spanish), Buenos Aires, Argentina.

Lichtwelle-Verlag – www.lichtwelle-verlag.ch (selected titles in Spanish and German), Zurich, Switzerland.

Shasti Association – www.shasti.org (selected titles in English), Mount Shasta, CA, USA

Lectures of Trigueirinho with Simultaneous English Translation

During over thirty years as Founder of the Figueira Community of Light, Trigueirinho gave bi-weekly lectures (called 'parthilha's or 'sharings') that were recorded live. Audience members were invited to submit questions to him which were placed in a small box and brought to him by an attendant. Arriving early, Trigueirinho sat at the lectern, reading through and taking notes on the audience questions. Thus, his lectures often began with the phrase "someone has asked a question...." After addressing some of these questions, he continued with the theme chosen for the day.

Approximately 70 of these 'sharings' were later dubbed with English translations. His voice or the translators can be augmented or diminished by adjusting the right-left balance of the recording.

To access these audio recordings go to: www.shasti.org/instruction, then drop down the menu tab titled "Trigueirinho Instruction" and then click on "MP3 audios."

A Book to Be Written
A New Viewpoint of the Monad
Alopathic and Homeopathic Medicine
An Esoteric Dimension of Power
An Overview of Current Life
Angels and Humanity – 1
Angels and Humanity – 2
Angels and Humanity – 3
Angels and Humanity – 4
Bases of the Fiery World
Beyond Fire by Friction
Beyond Imperfection
Causal Body
Colors in Healing and the Formation of Our Light Vessel
Deep Healing
From the Human Kingdom to the Spiritual Kingdom
Getting through Today's Critical Times
Harmonization and Androgyny
How One Begins to Perceive One's Inner Self
How to Understand the Planetary Disasters
Human Trials | The Trials of the Soul
Information on the New Earth and the New Humanity
Inner and Outer Figueira
Instruction: a Step beyond Teaching
Liberating and Healing through Colors
Life in Cosmic Signs
New Supraterrestrial Pathways – 1
New Supraterrestrial Pathways – 2
New Supraterrestrial Pathways – 3
New Supraterrestrial Pathways – 4
Niskalkat
Noah's Vessel
On Vitality
Our Response to the Cosmos – 1
Our Response to the Cosmos – 2
Our Response to the Cosmos – 3
Our Response to the Cosmos – 4
Our Response to the Cosmos – 5
Our Response to the Cosmos – 6
Preparation for the Path of Initiation
Reflections on Illusion and Rescue
Reflections on Inner Attunement
Seeds of Inner Transformation
Seeking to Understand the Self

Several Levels of Spiritual Reading
Special Paths and the Path of the Majority
Spiritual Entities and Hierarchies
Spiritual Trials
Strengthening the Bases for the New Cycles
Subtle Bodies and Templing
Supraterrestrial Pathways – 1
Supraterrestrial Pathways – 2
Supraterrestrial Pathways – 3
Supraterrestrial Pathways – 4
Syntheses, Struggles and New Instructions
Taking Charge of One's Process of Dying – 1
Taking Charge of One's Process of Dying – 2
Taking Charge of One's Process of Dying – 3
The Art of Living in Current Times
The Cosmic Signs Reveal the Teaching – 1
The Cosmic Signs Reveal the Teaching – 2
The Desert
The Earth – Degeneration and Deliverance
The Era of the Gigantic Wave
The Importance of Self-Control in Epidemics
  and Other Risk Situations
The Light That Permeates Matter
The Mystery of the Cross in the Present
  Planetary Transition
The Doorways of the Planet – 1
The Doorways of the Planet – 2
The Doorways of the Planet – 3
The Doorways of the Planet – 4
The Doorways of the Planet – 5
The Days of Tomorrow
The Heart, the Ego and the Personality
The New Life That is Emerging
The Plan of Evolution and Us
The Practical Mystic
The Seventh Ray and the Devas
The Spark from the Divine Level
The Transmutation of the Logos of the Earth
The Voice of Amhaj
To Be Universal – Part 1
To Be Universal – Part 2

To Medical Doctors and Therapists
To Those Who Pray – 1
To Those Who Pray – 2
Towards Self Consecration
We are Part of the Cosmos
Working Spiritually with One's Mind
Working with the Feminine Polarity
Working with the Rays